Roycemore School

W9-BYO-726

THE BASICS OF
MAGNETISM

THE **BASICS** OF
MAGNETISM

CHRISTOPHER COOPER

ROSEN
PUBLISHING®

New York

This edition published in 2015 by:

The Rosen Publishing Group, Inc.
29 East 21st Street
New York, NY 10010

Additional end matter copyright © 2015 by The Rosen Publishing Group, Inc.

Library of Congress Cataloging-in-Publication Data

Cooper, Christopher.
The basics of magnetism/by Christopher Cooper.
    p. cm.—(Core concepts)
Includes bibliographic references and index.
ISBN 978-1-4777-7760-2 (library binding)
1. Magnetism—Juvenile literature. 2. Magnets—Juvenile literature. I. Cooper, Christopher (Christopher E.). II. Title.
QC753.7 C66 2015
538—d23

Manufactured in the United States of America

© 2004 Brown Bear Books Ltd.

CONTENTS

CHAPTER ONE

MAGIC OR MAGNET?

A magnetic rock called lodestone has a power that seemed magical to early people. It can point to the north and guide a traveler even when all landmarks are hidden by night or in bad weather. Early explorers used this "magic" on sea voyages.

Among the Earth's many types of rock is a very unusual one, first recognized perhaps as early as 2700 B.C. by Chinese scholars. This rock, called lodestone (or magnetite, to give it its modern name), contains iron. It attracts other metals, and pieces of it will either attract or repel each other depending on how they are oriented.

The magnetic compass was used by Arab traders, who sailed in boats called dhows, like this one, along the shores of the Indian Ocean, southward to East Africa and eastward to India.

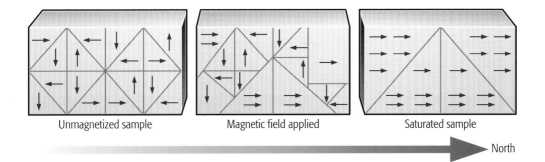

Unmagnetized sample   Magnetic field applied   Saturated sample

North

MAGNETIC DOMAINS

Tiny areas in a piece of iron, called domains, are like individual magnets. Applying a magnetic field lines up these magnets. The metal is said to be saturated when all the domains have their magnetism lined up.

Lodestone demonstrates another amazing property when it is set up so that it can turn freely. It will turn until it is pointing roughly north–south. This magnetic "compass" may have been used by navigators as early as the 3rd century in China. Certainly it was in use by European sailors in the 12th century.

Supplies of lodestone were limited. But it was possible to use a piece of lodestone to make a large number of magnetic needles for use in compasses. By stroking an iron needle with the lodestone many times, always in the same direction, the iron became magnetized.

In the 20th century this effect was explained. Individual atoms of iron and other elements present in a piece of metal are like miniature magnets. The metal is divided into regions called domains in which all the atoms line up. The magnetism of the atoms adds together, making each domain into a tiny magnet. But the atoms in different domains point in different directions, so that overall the piece of metal does not behave like a magnet. Repeated stroking with a piece of lodestone causes the atoms to turn. Eventually they all point in the same direction, and their magnetism adds up to make the whole piece of metal a strong magnet. When all the atoms are lined up and the magnetism cannot become any greater, the piece of metal is said to be saturated.

A magnetic needle enables this portable sundial to be aligned north–south to take a correct reading. The instrument also doubles as a magnetic compass.

A hiker uses a magnetic compass to find the direction of a landmark. She can correct the reading if she knows the angle between magnetic north and true north.

CHAPTER TWO

SPHERES OF INFLUENCE

Surrounding a magnet and extending into nearby space is a "sphere of influence" called a magnetic field. How another magnet is affected by the first magnet depends both on this magnetic field and on the second magnet's own properties.

A piece of lodestone or other magnet will attract small metal objects to itself. The way they arrange themselves around the magnet reveals to us important facts about magnetism. Iron filings—tiny metal grains produced when a block of iron is filed or machined—show this especially clearly. They cluster around the two ends of a bar magnet, but not toward its middle. If the magnet is in the shape of a horseshoe, the filings cluster at the ends of the two "legs," but not around its middle. Every magnet has these two "attractive ends," called its poles.

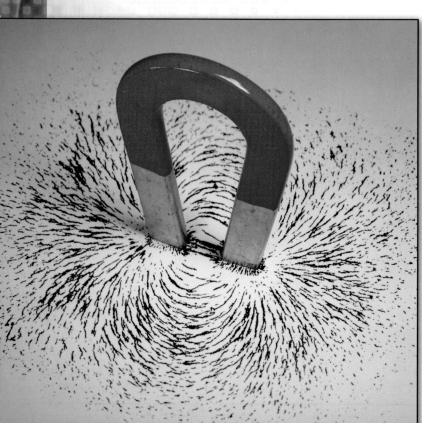

Iron filings scattered around the poles of a horseshoe magnet reveal the magnetic field around them. Each filing orients itself in the direction of the field at its location, and together they trace a dramatic picture of the whole magnetic field.

One of the poles of a magnet is attracted to the north and the other to the south—that is why a compass needle swings until it is pointing north–south. The north-seeking pole is called the magnet's north, or N, pole; the south-seeking pole is the south, or S, pole.

OPPOSITES ATTRACT

When the two north poles of a magnet are brought close to each other, they can be felt to repel each other. The closer together they are, the harder is the mutual push. The same happens if the two south poles are brought close to each other. But when a north pole is brought close to a south pole, a force of attraction can be felt. Again, the force is stronger the closer the poles are to each other.

The field can be "mapped" with the aid of a small compass. If it is brought close to a magnet, the needle of the compass points toward or

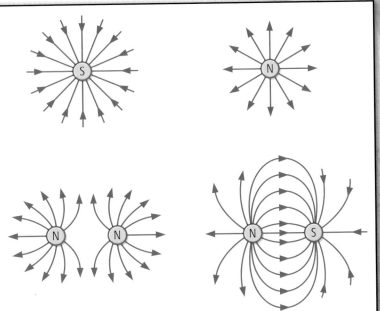

ONE OR TWO POLES

These fields are produced by one or two magnetic poles. Such poles always occur in linked pairs, but if they are widely separated, they can be regarded as single poles.

PLOTTING THE FIELD

Trails of dots marking successive positions of the head and tail of the compass needle trace out field lines.

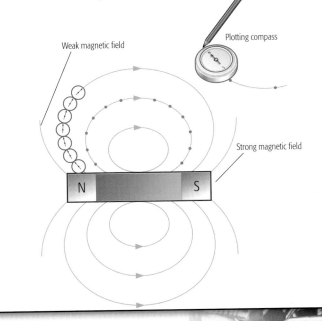

Weak magnetic field

Plotting compass

Strong magnetic field

N   S

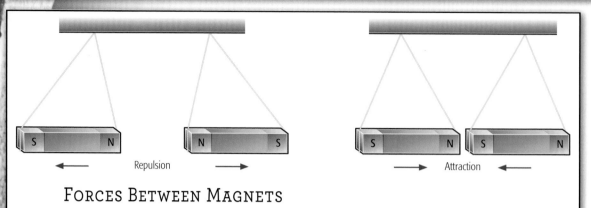

FORCES BETWEEN MAGNETS

Two bar magnets suspended on strings will push each other apart or pull each other together depending on whether like poles (two N or two S) or unlike poles (N and S) are closest to each other.

away from the nearest pole of the magnet. If the nearest pole is a south pole, the north-seeking end of the needle points toward it. If the compass is moved toward the other end of the magnet, the effect of the north pole gradually increases, and the needle turns until its south-seeking end points toward the north pole.

To map the field, put the magnet on a piece of paper and place the compass anywhere on the paper. Mark the two ends of the needle with pencil dots. Then move the compass until the tail of the needle is just over the dot that marks the previous position of the head of the needle. Mark the new position of the head of

FIELD LINES

Field lines, or lines of force, are imaginary lines showing the force that the magnet would exert on an imaginary north magnetic pole. At each point the direction of the field line shows the direction of the force.

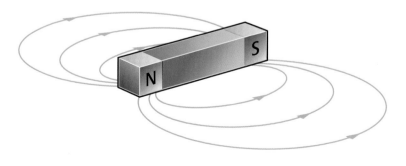

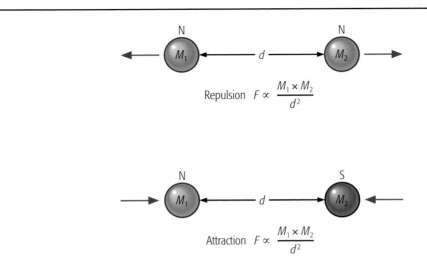

$$\text{Repulsion} \quad F \propto \frac{M_1 \times M_2}{d^2}$$

$$\text{Attraction} \quad F \propto \frac{M_1 \times M_2}{d^2}$$

A FORCE BETWEEN POLES

Two north poles repel each other, as do two south poles. A north and a south pole attract each other. The force between two magnetic poles is proportional to M_1 and M_2, the strengths of the magnets, and inversely proportional to d_2, the square of the distance between them.

the needle, and again move the compass until the tail of the needle is at that position. Continue repeating this process.

The result is a chain of dots that can be joined up smoothly to make a curved line. At every point along this line the direction of the line is the direction of the compass at that point, which is the direction of the force that would be experienced by any magnetic object at that point. The curved line is called a line of force or a field line. The region in which magnetic forces are experienced is the magnetic field. Field lines indicate the north–south direction.

SEEING MAGNETIC FIELDS

The magnetic field can also be made visible in a striking way with the aid of iron filings. If a sheet of paper is placed over a magnet and iron filings are shaken over the paper, many cluster directly over the poles. But some lie scattered over the rest of the area around the magnet and arrange themselves in curved lines. The lines run from one pole to the other. They are formed as each individual grain lines up in a certain direction. Each grain acts like a tiny magnetic compass and points in a definite direction. Together they give

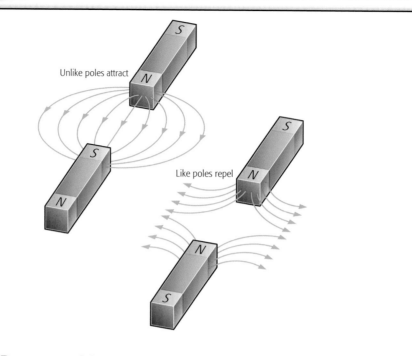

FIELDS BETWEEN MAGNETS

When two bar magnets are brought near each other, the shapes of the field lines between them depend on which poles are involved.

a vivid picture of the form of the field, and even of its strength, for the lines crowd together near poles, where the field is strongest. The more the field lines spread out, the weaker the field is.

The direction of the field at a point is defined as the direction of the force that would be experienced by the north pole of another magnet at that point. According to this definition, the field lines run outside the magnet from its north pole toward its south pole. Entering the magnet near the south pole, they return toward the north pole, each forming a closed loop. Field lines do not normally meet or cross one another.

MEASURING STRENGTH

Every magnet has two opposite poles: no isolated pole is known to exist. (Physicists have made searches for subatomic particles that are single magnetic poles, but such "monopoles" have never been discovered.) This makes working out the laws of the magnetic field difficult. It is easier to see what is happening with a very long bar magnet, with the poles far apart. The magnetic effects of each pole can then be studied while the influence of the other one is ignored.

The strength of the magnetic field produced by a single pole can be measured at each point in space by measuring the force on another magnetic pole placed there. It is found that the strength of the field falls to one-fourth when the distance is doubled, to one-ninth when it is tripled, to one-sixteenth when it is increased four-fold, and so on. That is to say, the field strength is inversely proportional to the square of the distance. (Many other physical quantities also fall off in strength as the square of the distance, including the strength of gravity and of electrical fields, and the brightness of light.)

The strength of the magnetic field at a given point depends not only on how far from the magnet that point is but also on the strength of the magnet itself. A particular piece of iron, for example, can be more or less strongly magnetized. (The word "magnetic" describes a material that can be made into a magnet whether or not it is a magnet now. The word "magnetized" refers to a magnetic material that actually is a magnet.) Magnetic materials include iron, cobalt, and nickel, and alloys such as steel. Scientists have also created nonmetalic materials called ferrites that can be made into powerful magnets.

Holding two magnets together lets you feel the force of the attraction or repulsion.

CHAPTER THREE

OUR MAGNETIC EARTH

We live on a giant magnet. The turning of the Earth's core generates our planet's magnetic field, which not only influences compasses but reaches far into space. It changes slowly with time, and the record of these changes is written in the rocks, revealing the planet's geological history billions of years into the past.

The Earth's magnetic field is like that of a huge bar magnet deep within the planet and aligned quite closely with the Earth's axis of rotation. The poles of this imaginary magnet lie beneath two opposite points on the Earth's surface, close to the geographical poles, where the field lines are vertical. The points on the surface are called the Earth's north and south magnetic poles. The magnetic equator is the imaginary line around the Earth, halfway between the magnetic poles, where the field lines are horizontal.

Because a magnetic compass points to the magnetic poles, it does not in general point to true north or true south. The angle between true north and "magnetic north" is

Shifting, multicolored auroras are often seen in the sky in polar regions. They are caused by electrically charged particles, mostly from the Sun, being funneled by the Earth's magnetic field down from space toward the magnetic poles.

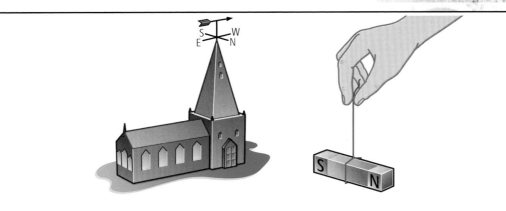

SEEKING NORTH

When it can turn freely, a bar magnet swings until it points north–south. The magnet's poles are called north and south, according to which direction they point in.

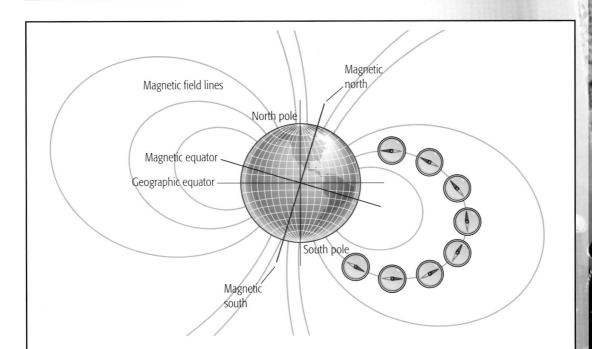

THE EARTH AS A MAGNET

The lines of force of the Earth's magnetic field can be traced just as they can for a small magnet. The field has the same shape as the magnetic field of a bar magnet. The north magnetic pole lies about 1,300 km (800 miles) from the geographical north pole. The south magnetic pole is about twice as far as this from the geographical south pole.

called variation. The direction of magnetic north is shown on some maps. Variation changes with time because the positions of the poles change: they wander by about 20 km (12 miles) per year.

ANIMAL ATTRACTION

Many types of animal rely, at least partly, on the Earth's magnetism to guide them. Some birds migrate from one continent to another at the beginning of summer and winter. They get their sense of direction largely from the position of the Sun or stars; but when the skies are cloudy and they cannot do that, their sense of the Earth's magnetism guides them. Water-dwelling organisms that are sensitive to the Earth's magnetic field include some bacteria, whales, dolphins, sharks, and sea turtles.

MAGNETOSPHERE AND HELIOSPHERE

The Earth's magnetic field extends into space. Electrically charged particles that constantly flow outward from the Sun are called the solar wind. They are trapped by the Earth's magnetic field and form two thick belts of charged particles, known as the Van Allen belts.

The Earth's magnetosphere is the volume of space in which the Earth's magnetic field is stronger than that of the Sun. The solar wind squeezes the magnetosphere, so that it is 64,000 km (40,000 miles) above the surface on the sunward side of the Earth, but stretches into a tail, over 1 million km (600,000 miles) long, on the side away from the Sun. Some other planets, in particular Jupiter, possess magnetic fields and magnetospheres. The Sun's magnetic field is very powerful and dominates a region of space, called the heliosphere, extending beyond the distant dwarf planet Pluto.

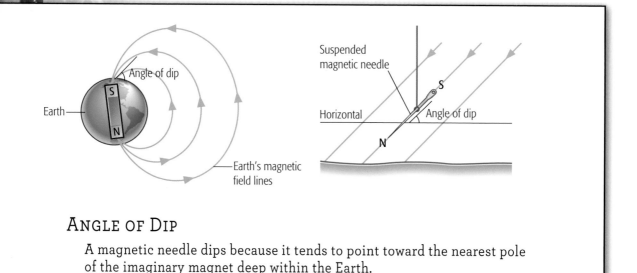

ANGLE OF DIP

A magnetic needle dips because it tends to point toward the nearest pole of the imaginary magnet deep within the Earth.

WILLIAM GILBERT

An English physician and scientist, William Gilbert, made the discovery that the Earth is a gigantic magnet. Born in 1544, he published his book *De Magnete* ("On the Magnet") in 1600. In it he explained that the Earth had a magnetic field resembling that of a bar magnet. He investigated variation and magnetic dip. Gilbert also studied electricity, and conjectured that electricity and magnetism are closely related. Among his other scientific contributions he supported the theory that the Sun, and not the Earth, is the center of the Universe. Queen Elizabeth I made Gilbert her personal physician in 1601. He died in 1603.

CONTINENTAL DRIFT

Although lodestone is the only strongly magnetized rock, many other types of rock were weakly magnetized when they were formed. The direction of their magnetic field was the same as that of the Earth at that time, but since then the rocks have moved. By patient detective work it is possible to reconstruct how the rocks have moved since their formation. This work shows that the continents have drifted over the surface of the Earth ever since a single supercontinent called Pangaea broke up about 180 million years ago.

FIELD REVERSALS

Electric currents in the Earth's molten outer core generate its magnetic field. In addition to the slow changes in direction of the field that cause "polar wandering," every few hundred thousand years the field dies down to zero and then increases in strength again, now pointing in the opposite direction. The record of these field reversals is written in the magnetism of the rocks.

CHAPTER FOUR

HOW TO MAKE A MAGNET

Magnets were precious objects in societies that relied on them for navigation. Practical people learned methods of making magnets from iron and steel. Nowadays we have effective ways of making the very strong magnets that various devices rely on.

It was probably in ancient times when people discovered that hammering an iron bar while it is aligned north–south magnetizes it. If the iron is made red-hot and allowed to cool while being hammered, it gets even more strongly magnetized.

Stroking a piece of iron with a magnet also magnetizes it. Sailors used to take a piece of lodestone on voyages so that they could "refresh" their compass needles, or magnetize new ones, whenever it was necessary. Hammering an iron bar could provide a substitute for the lodestone.

These methods of magnetizing the metal depend on the fact that a piece of unmagnetized iron or steel is made up of countless tiny magnets—the domains, or regions where atoms are all aligned (see page 7). Because they are pointing in all directions, these domains cancel one

A simple electromagnet can be made with a battery, a nail, and some wire.

MAKING MAGNETS

1. Using another magnet

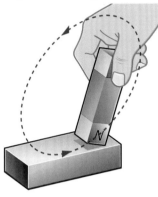

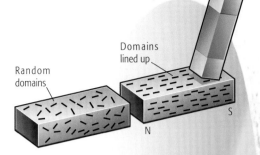

You can make a magnet from a steel bar by stroking it repeatedly with a bar magnet. In unmagnetized steel the magnetic domains point in all directions. Their north and south poles cancel each other out. Stroking the steel with a bar magnet pulls the domains around so that they are pointing in the same direction. The steel is now magnetized.

2. Hitting the metal

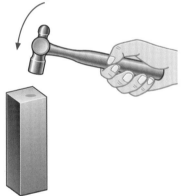

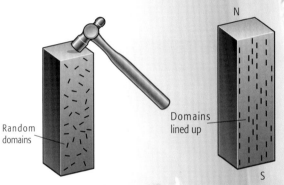

Hammering an iron bar gradually magnetizes it. Polar explorers used to do this when their supply of lodestone lost its magnetism and would no longer magnetize compass needles. The domains in the iron bar are jumbled to begin with. With the hammer blows they gradually turn, pulled by the Earth's field (nearly vertical in polar regions). Finally, the domains are lined up parallel to the Earth's field, and a magnet has been formed.

3. Using a coil

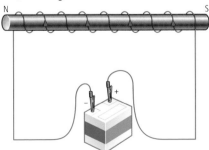

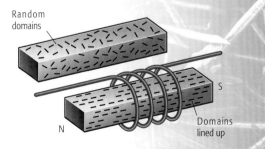

Applying a magnetic field generated by an electric current for a long time can also magnetize an iron bar. The domains remain lined up, though possibly only weakly, after the current is turned off.

another out, and the metal has no overall magnetization. To turn the metal into a magnet, the atoms in all the domains have to be rotated so that they all point the same way.

A very strong magnetic field can do this. A coil of wire carrying an electric current can provide such a field (see chapter seven). The moderate field of another magnet that is made to stroke the piece of metal repeatedly can also magnetize the metal. If the north pole of the magnet makes contact with the metal being magnetized, it will pull the south poles of the atomic magnets toward itself. A south pole will develop at the end of the metal where the magnet breaks contact.

The Earth's magnetic field is strong enough to align the atoms and magnetize the metal if the atoms are constantly disturbed by hammer blows or by being heated. (Heat makes a metal's atoms vibrate more vigorously.) The opposite is also true. Heating a magnet or repeatedly

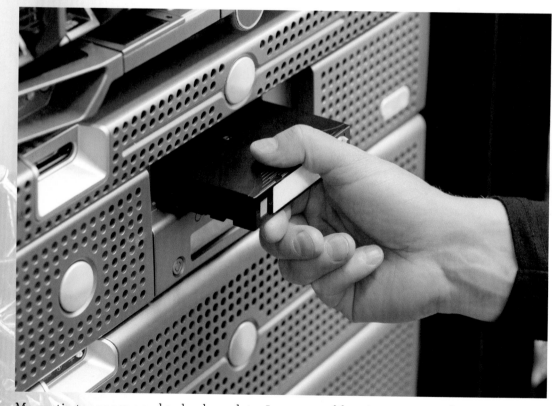

Magnetic tapes are used to back up data. Large tape libraries can store thousands of times the amount of data stored on a typical computer hard drive.

Coming into contact with a powerful magnet can completely erase the hard drive of a computer.

striking it with a hammer "shakes up" the atomic magnets. They take on a random arrangement again, and the magnet loses its magnetism.

Objects left for a long period near a magnet can become magnetized. The loudspeakers of audio equipment contain strong permanent magnets. Small metal objects such as screws can become magnetized if they are left a long time near speakers. Being left near speakers can spoil audiotapes (on which sound is recorded as a pattern of magnetization in the metal coating on a plastic tape) because the magnetization is altered. Stray magnetic fields can also affect other types of magnetic storage device, such as videotapes and computer hard drives.

CHAPTER FIVE

PUTTING MAGNETS TO WORK

Magnets, often working hand in hand with electricity, are essential in recording, transmitting, and receiving data in audio, TV, and computer systems. In industry they do heavy work, while in medicine they reveal the workings of our bodies.

Magnets are used in devices all around us. One important use is in computers. Computers use many sorts of storage devices. One example is the hard disk. Hard disks are rigid and coated with magnetic material. Data is stored in this coating by a moving arm called a read–write head, which applies a magnetic field to the disk to make a tiny magnetized area, corresponding to a bit. (A bit is a 0 or a 1, the basic units of

A computer's hard disk drive contains two or more rigid metal platters coated with a magnetic material. Read-write heads swing back and forth across each platter as it spins rapidly.

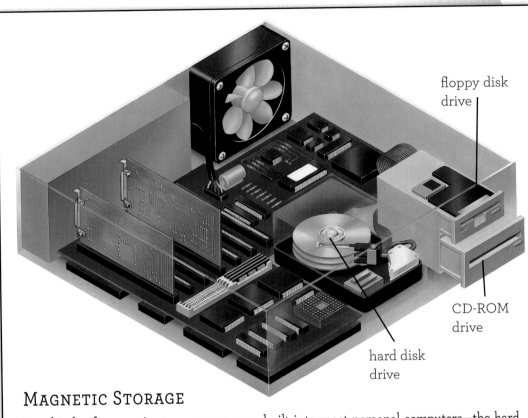

floppy disk drive

CD-ROM drive

hard disk drive

MAGNETIC STORAGE

Two kinds of magnetic storage were once built into most personal computers—the hard drive, using one or more hard disks, and the "floppy" disk drive, using a single flexible magnetic disk. Today's CD-ROM and DVD drives are nonmagnetic.

information as used in connection with computers and digital communications.) The read–write head can also read information already on the disk by detecting the magnetization of the surface directly beneath the head.

Some large mainframe computers, which have to store large quantities of information, also use magnetic tapes. These consist of plastic film with a coating of a magnetic material. The same principle is used in audiotapes and videotapes for storing information representing sounds and pictures.

A magnetic signal is recorded onto a magnetic disk or tape by applying a fluctuating magnetic field. A varying electric current flowing through an electromagnet in the recording head creates this field. When the magnetic signal is read,

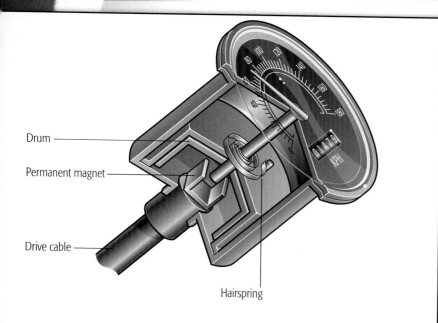

Drum

Permanent magnet

Drive cable

Hairspring

MAGNETIC SPEEDOMETER

The drive cable is turned by the vehicle's gearbox and spins the permanent magnet inside a drum. The drum is made of a magnetic material but is not magnetized. The spinning magnet drags the drum around against the resistance of the hairspring. The angle by which the drum turns indicates the speed of the vehicle.

the fluctuations in the magnetism of the recording surface as it speeds past the detector generate a varying electric current in the detector. This current is then amplified to give the output.

TAKING PICTURES

Modern medicine now relies heavily on the ability to create images of organs inside the living human body. There

are several techniques for doing this, and one of the most important is magnetic resonance imaging (MRI).

When a patient has an MRI scan, he or she lies down and is positioned with the relevant part of the body, such as the head or chest, in the scanner. A powerful magnetic field, tens of thousands of times as strong as the Earth's field, is turned on. The patient's body is then bathed in radio waves. The magnetic field puts the hydrogen atoms in the patient's tissues into a state in which they can absorb energy from the radio waves. When the signals are turned off, these hydrogen atoms reradiate the energy they have absorbed. Detectors pick up these "broadcasts," and a powerful computer assembles the signals into a multicolored image of the interior of the body. The brightness and color of each part of the image represent the amount and type of tissue present at the corresponding point in the body.

A technique called functional MRI (fMRI) can show how much activity is going on in a person's internal organs—for example, the activity of the

Magnetic Separater

Magnetic and nonmagnetic scrap metals can be separated from each other by means of a rotating drum and an electromagnet. Copper and brass are among the metals that simply slide off the drum. Iron, steel, and other magnetic metals stick to its surface until they pass the magnet and fall off.

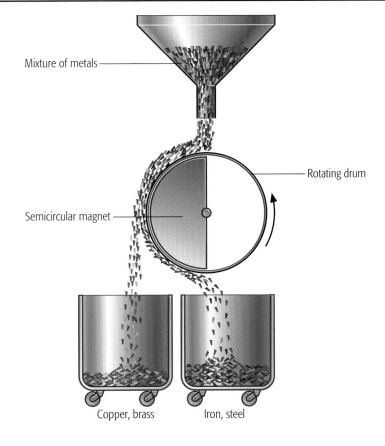

Mixture of metals

Rotating drum

Semicircular magnet

Copper, brass

Iron, steel

parts of the brain that are involved in emotional reactions or in tasks such as mental arithmetic.

LIFTING AND SORTING

Electromagnets are important in industry. They are magnets in which the magnetism is generated by electric current. The magnetic field can be much stronger than is possible in solid permanent magnets, and it can be switched on and off simply by switching the current on and off (see chapter seven). Electromagnets are used in cranes for lifting iron and steel objects, such as junked vehicles at wrecking yards.

They can also be used for separating metal ores and scrap metal. This is an essential preliminary to processing them in order to get a high level of purity in the metal that is refined from the ore or recovered from the scrap. The materials to be separated are dropped onto a

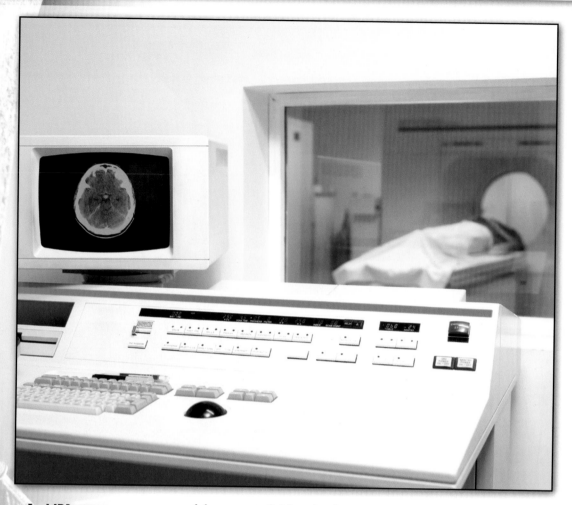

An MRI scanner uses a powerful magnetic field and radio waves to make hydrogen atoms in the patient's body "broadcast" their own radio signals, from which a computer can build up an image of the patient's internal organs.

drum rotating around a semicircular electromagnet. Any nonmagnetic materials drop off into a bin. The drum holds magnetic materials as it rotates until they pass the magnet, when they fall into a separate container.

GUIDE AND COLLIDE

Scientists learn about the structure of matter by accelerating subatomic particles in giant machines called colliders and then smashing the particles into one another. Two such machines share an enormous circular underground tunnel

27 km (17 miles) in circumference at CERN, the European Laboratory for Particle Physics, near Geneva, in Switzerland. To keep the particles, traveling at almost the speed of light, on the curved path, they have to be held on course by electromagnets that encircle the path of the particle beams. The electromagnets have to be very powerful, and for this purpose superconductors are used. They are metals kept at low temperatures so that they become superconducting—that is, they pass electric currents without offering any electrical resistance and therefore lose almost no energy as wasted heat.

Computer servers generally need more memory and storage capacity. They are often stored in separate rooms, called server rooms, where they are secure and the temperature and climate can be controlled.

Magnetic fields are also important in the detectors that record the paths of particles produced in the collisions. A magnetic field forces the electrically charged particles to follow curved paths. The amount of curvature depends on the speed of the particle and on its mass. So a magnetic field is generated in a particle detector to bend the paths of the particles produced. Measuring the curvatures of the paths that appear in the pictures gives important information about the particles.

Magnetic fields also bend the paths of particles in TV sets. Electromagnets in the picture tube force a beam of electrons to sweep from side to side and from top to bottom of the screen, making dots of phosphorescent material glow and form a picture.

These large superconducting electromagnets are part of CERN's Large Hadron Collider. Opened in 2008, it is the world's largest and most powerful particle collider.

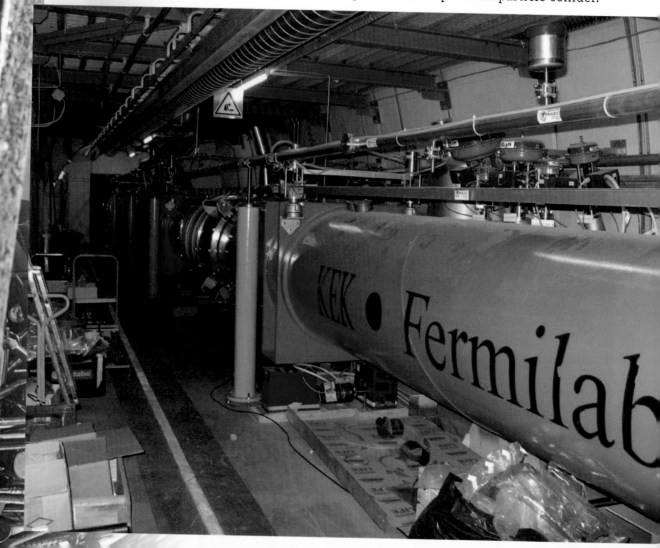

Once scrap metals have been sorted, they can be melted down to make other products. Using scrap metal instead of new metal ores saves energy and water and reduces air and water pollution.

CHAPTER SIX

UNDERSTANDING ELECTROMAGNETISM

For nearly 200 years scientists have known that electricity and magnetism are closely interlinked. Electric currents generate magnetic fields; and magnetic fields, when they alter, can drive electric currents. Scientists now regard electricity and magnetism as two aspects of a single phenomenon, which is called electromagnetism.

The link between electricity and magnetism was first discovered quite early in the 19th century. Hans Christian

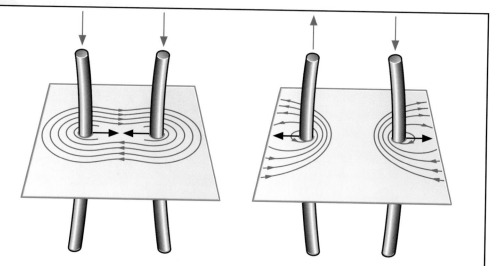

MAGNETIC FIELDS OF CURRENTS

The magnetic field lines around a current-carrying wire are circular. With current flowing downward into a surface, the field lines run clockwise as seen from above. The fields of nearby currents combine in the patterns shown here. When the currents in two parallel wires are in the same direction, the wires attract each other. When they are in opposite directions, the wires repel each other.

Oersted (see page 35) found that a wire carrying an electric current will affect a magnetic needle. The magnetic field lines around a wire are circles. If you look along a wire, and the current is flowing toward you, the field lines (the direction of the force on a north magnetic pole) go in a counterclockwise sense, as shown in diagram (a) below. (Throughout this book the direction of an electric current is defined as the direction of flow of positive charge. Actually, the current consists of negatively charged electrons moving in the opposite direction, but this does not really matter.)

This looks very different from the shape of the field of a bar magnet or of the Earth. But if the wire is coiled into a single loop, the shape of the field begins to resemble that of a bar magnet (b, opposite). And if the wire is looped into many turns to form a cylindrical coil, called a solenoid (c and d), the fields of all the loops combine to make a stronger field, and the field lines strongly resemble those of a bar magnet.

In fact, the field of a magnetic material is created by countless tiny electric currents in the atoms of metal forming myriad tiny magnets, which act in unison to form the one big magnet.

The magnetic fields of electric currents interact with each other just as the magnetic fields of magnets do. The result

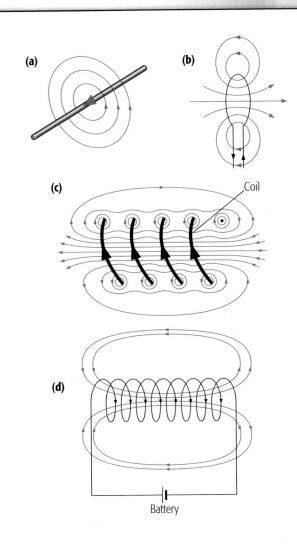

(a)

(b)

(c)   Coil

(d)

Battery

CURRENT-CARRYING COILS

The field of a current (a) becomes more and more like that of a bar magnet as the wire is bent into more and more coils (b, c, and d).

is that electric currents attract and repel one another. As shown in the illustration on page 32, currents flowing in the same direction in two neighboring wires attract each other, while currents flowing in opposite directions repel each other. And solenoids behave just like bar magnets in this way, too: each has a north-seeking and a south-seeking end, or pole, and like poles repel while unlike ones attract.

At airports there are metal detectors to guard against concealed weapons and bombs in baggage or passengers' clothing. The devices respond to the magnetic effects of metal objects.

Hans Christian Oersted was the first person to produce the metal aluminum in 1825.

HANS CHRISTIAN OERSTED

In the 17th and 18th centuries scientists often compared the effects of magnetism with those of electricity. But the Danish physicist Hans Christian Oersted, born in 1777, was the first to discover a link experimentally. In 1819 he found that an electric current flowing in a wire would make a nearby magnetic needle swing. Among his other work in physics he made a very accurate measurement of the compressibility of water. Oersted was also a chemist and was the first person to isolate the metal aluminum. He died in 1851. A unit of magnetic field strength was named after him, but is not commonly used.

CHAPTER SEVEN

CREATING ELECTROMAGNETS

Electricity can be used to generate powerful magnetic fields that can be turned on and off at the flick of a switch. Electromagnets are valuable in industry, and the principle behind them is applied in countless other devices, many familiar in the home.

Coiling a current-carrying wire into a solenoid makes it into an electromagnet. This is a very convenient type of magnet because it can be switched on and off. The strength of its magnetism depends on the strength of the current passing through it. However, the amount of current is limited by the heating effect that it causes.

An electromagnet can be made more powerful by wrapping the wire around a central core of iron. It becomes strongly magnetized by the magnetic field of the solenoid, which greatly strengthens the total field of the magnet. As the strength

A powerful electromagnet suspended from the end of a crane's jib can lift tons of scrap metal.

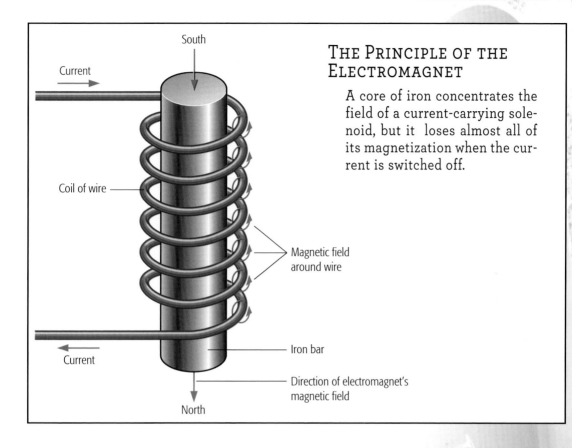

South

Current

Coil of wire

Magnetic field
around wire

Iron bar

Direction of electromagnet's
magnetic field

Current

North

THE PRINCIPLE OF THE ELECTROMAGNET

A core of iron concentrates the field of a current-carrying sole-noid, but it loses almost all of its magnetization when the current is switched off.

of the current is increased, the magnetization of the iron increases until it reaches a maximum—it becomes saturated (see page 7). Increasing the current further increases the field only by the amount contributed by the solenoid's own direct field. Whatever material is used in the electromagnet's core, it needs to be "soft," which means that it is able to lose magnetism as readily as it gains it.

The current required to power an electromagnet can come from any of several different sources. In portable devices such as electric razors, batteries do the job. On motor vehicles, ships, and airplanes the vehicle's own engine or engines generate an electrical supply that powers all the systems, including those that incorporate electromagnets. In homes, offices, and factories the electricity supply is the source of current (see chapter eight). In some of the first experiments to study electromagnets, the U.S. physicist Joseph Henry used a primitive electric cell, or battery. It consisted of plates of two different kinds of metal, such as copper and zinc, dipping into acid. Using hundreds of turns of insulated wire, Henry made electromagnets that could lift over a ton.

Here you can see a degaussing cable running along the length of the RMS *Queen Mary*, a large ocean liner that carried Allied troops during World War II.

DANGER AT SEA

One of the strangest ever applications of the electromagnet has been in wartime to protect ships against magnetic mines. Magnetic mines float beneath the surface of the sea, tethered to the sea floor. When a ship passes nearby, the metal of the ship is detected by a sensitive magnetic needle in the mine. The swinging needle acts as the moving part of an electric switch. If a nearby ship makes the needle swing, the switch is closed. Current from a battery flows through an electric detonator, exploding the mine and damaging or even sinking the ship.

The mine is triggered because the ship is a giant magnet, though a weak one, with a magnetic field induced by long exposure to the Earth's magnetic field. Degaussing belts—cables that encircle the ship's hull and carry electric current—generate a magnetic field opposite to that of the ship and in this way counteract the ship's own magnetism.

HENRY'S APPARATUS

Joseph Henry studied the lifting power of magnets with this apparatus. The horseshoe-shaped electromagnet A was supplied with current from a battery, B and C. He could measure the electromagnet's upward pull on the metal bar placed across its poles by seeing what weight it could support on the platform F, pulling down on the left-hand side of the arm D, counterbalanced by the weight E.

ELECTRON BEAMS

Electric currents are not confined to those that flow in wires. They also flow through free space. In a TV picture tube a beam of electrons travels from a heated cathode at the rear to sweep across the screen and illuminate tiny phosphor dots on the screen to form a picture. Beams of electrons are also used in electron microscopes, instruments that can see details far smaller than can be seen with optical

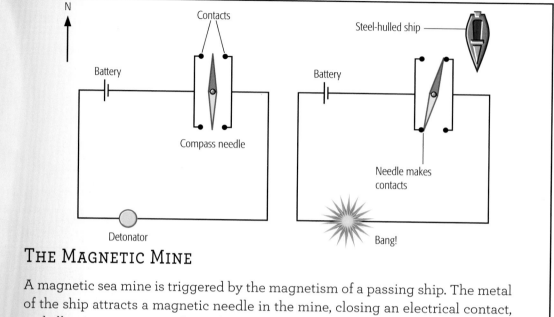

N

Contacts

Battery

Compass needle

Steel-hulled ship

Battery

Needle makes contacts

Detonator

Bang!

THE MAGNETIC MINE

A magnetic sea mine is triggered by the magnetism of a passing ship. The metal of the ship attracts a magnetic needle in the mine, closing an electrical contact, and allowing a current to flow, which detonates the explosive.

microscopes using ordinary light. One type of electron microscope, the transmission electron microscope, or TEM, can see details the size of individual atoms. The electrons are accelerated by hundreds of thousands of volts. (The electron beam current may be only a billionth of an ampere, compared with about half an ampere in the current going through a typical desk lamp bulb.) The electron beam is shaped, focused, and guided by electromagnets consisting of current-carrying coils through which the beam passes on the way to its target.

JOSEPH HENRY

The American physicist Joseph Henry was born in 1797. He discovered the principle of electromagnetic induction—that changing electric currents in one circuit can cause currents to be generated in another circuit. However, he did not get the credit for the discovery because the British physicist Michael Faraday announced the results of his own independent studies on the subject before Henry did. Henry developed improved electromagnets and built one of the first electric motors. He also invented one of the first successful electric telegraphs, for which he developed the relay, allowing messages to be sent over long distances without them growing fainter. In 1846 Henry became first director of the newly formed Smithsonian Institution in Washington, D.C., and served in that position until his death in 1878. He developed the study of meteorology at the Smithsonian and pioneered weather forecasting. The unit of electrical inductance is named in his honor.

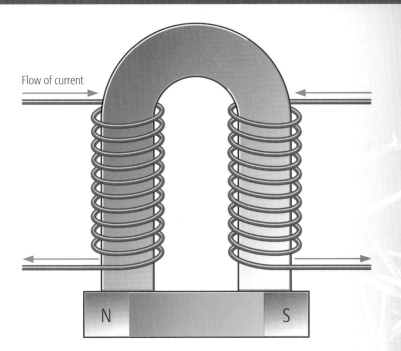

Flow of current

N   S

PRINCIPLE OF HENRY'S ELECTROMAGNET

Coils magnetize the two legs of the horseshoe magnet. The magnetism in each leg induces a magnetic pole at each end of a piece of iron placed across the horseshoe's poles.

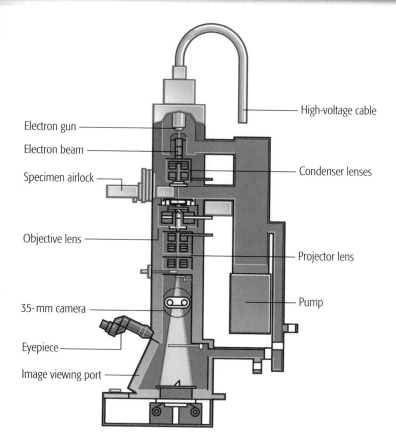

High-voltage cable

Electron gun

Electron beam

Specimen airlock

Condenser lenses

Objective lens

Projector lens

Pump

35-mm camera

Eyepiece

Image viewing port

ELECTRON MICROSCOPE

The electron microscope uses a beam of electrons in place of a beam of light. The electrons, like all subatomic particles, have a wavelength, which is much shorter than that of light, thus making it possible to form extremely detailed images. The electron beam, traveling from the top of the instrument downward, is focused by strong "magnetic lenses," which are current-carrying coils.

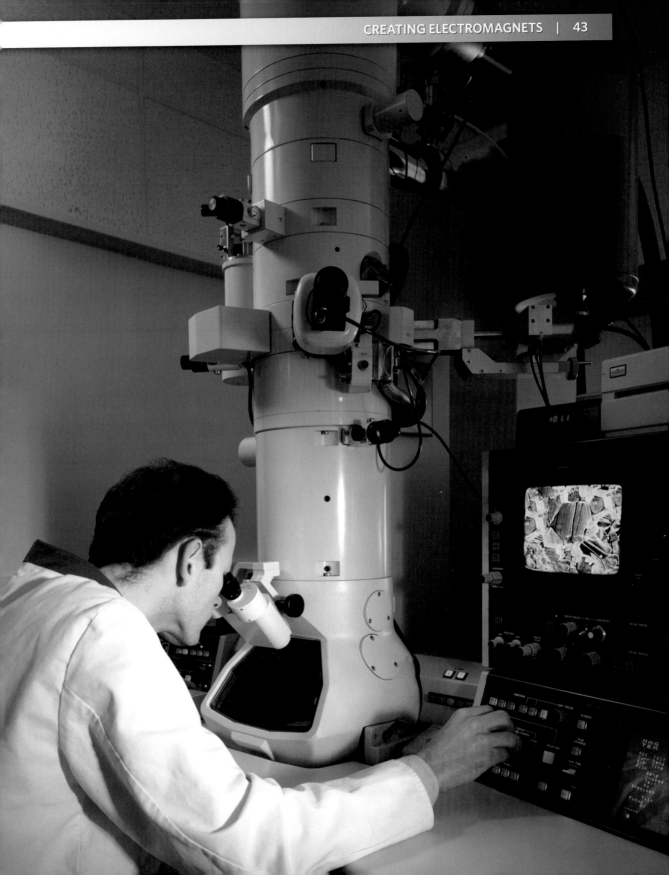

CHAPTER EIGHT

ELECTROMAGNETS IN ACTION

We live in a push-button world—we consider it normal that the press of a finger is enough to lift mighty weights, set great machines in motion, and carry our words around the world. All this is made possible by putting electromagnetism to work.

The discovery of electromagnetism by scientists in the early 19th century led to a steady stream of inventions that depended on the principle of electric currents and magnetic fields interacting with each other. The stream grew into a flood, and today we are surrounded by electromagnetic devices in daily life. The American physicist Joseph Henry made one of the earliest such innovations in 1831, when he built the first electric bell. The bell was struck repeatedly by a clapper that was held away from the bell by a spring when no current flowed. Pressing a button allowed electric current to flow in the circuit through a solenoid. The

The electric bell creates its high-pitched trilling noise by the action of a hammer striking the bell rapidly and repeatedly. The hammer vibrates because it is pulled one way by an electromagnet and the other way by a mechanical spring.

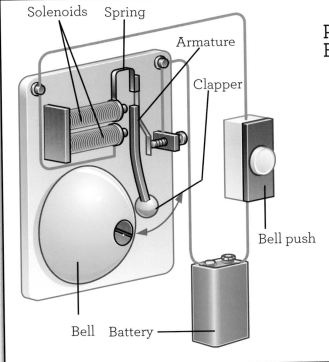

Solenoids Spring

Armature

Clapper

Bell push

Bell Battery

PRINCIPLE OF THE ELECTRIC BELL

When the current flows, the solenoids attract the armature and clapper. This strikes the bell, but its movement also breaks the circuit. The armature is immediately pulled back by the spring to its starting position.

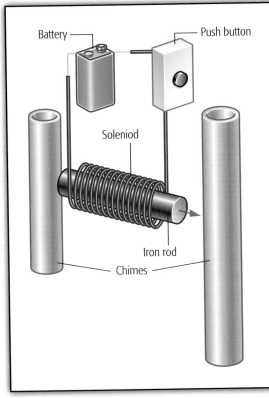

Battery

Push button

Soleniod

Iron rod

Chimes

DOOR CHIMES

Pressing the doorbell sends a pulse of current through the solenoid, making the iron rod jerk across sharply and hit one of the chimes. Instantly a spring (not shown) pulls it back again, striking the second chime.

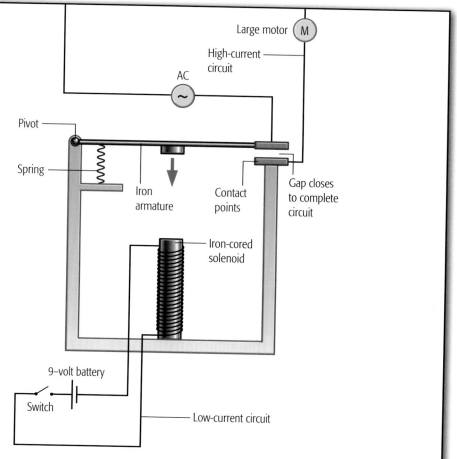

Large motor (M)

High-current circuit

AC

~

Pivot

Spring

Iron armature

Contact points

Gap closes to complete circuit

Iron-cored solenoid

9–volt battery

Switch

Low-current circuit

THE RELAY

A relay is a device by which the current in one circuit controls the current in a second circuit. In the design shown here a switch in a low-current circuit controls a motor that draws a large current. Closing the switch in the lower circuit allows a low current to pass, so that the solenoid generates a magnetic field. That attracts the pivoted armature, allowing a strong AC current to flow in the second circuit, operating the motor.

magnetic field generated by the solenoid attracted the metal arm of the clapper, which struck the bell sharply. But the movement of the clapper also broke the circuit so that the current ceased and the magnetic field disappeared. The clapper,

no longer attracted, jumped back and closed the circuit.

As long as the button was pressed, this cycle repeated itself, giving rise to the characteristic trilling sound of the electric bell. The electric bell was much more convenient than the pull-cord bell then in use. Electric wires could be run from room to room more easily than pull-cords and could be made to sound more than one bell if needed. Bells could be very loud and have a variety of tones. Variants such as chimes could easily be provided.

MESSAGES BY WIRE

An early use of electromagnetism was in the electric telegraph. Messages could be sent long distances by wire in the form of long and short pulses of electric current. These pulses would deflect a recording pen installed at the receiving end.

The short electric pulses corresponded to dots, and the long pulses to dashes. Combinations of dots and dashes stood for letters of the alphabet according to an international code devised by the American inventor Samuel Morse.

To send signals over long distances, it was necessary to overcome the weakening of signals as they passed over telegraph wires many kilometers long. Electromagnetism was put to use again with the invention of the relay. The signals in each stretch of telegraph wire, roughly 30 km (20 miles) long, were used to open and close switches in the next stretch of the wire, which had its own electricity supply. So the signals were

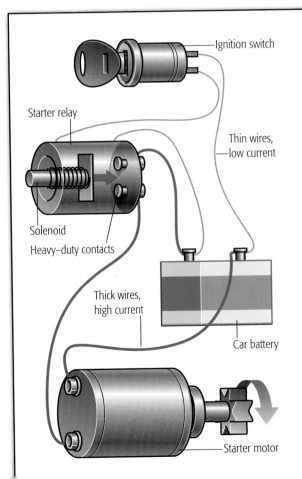

Ignition switch

Starter relay

Thin wires, low current

Solenoid

Heavy–duty contacts

Thick wires, high current

Car battery

Starter motor

STARTER MOTOR

A car is equipped with an electric starter motor, which is turned by a large current delivered to it by the car's battery. This current is turned on by the starter relay, in which a low current from the battery activates a solenoid when the driver turns the key in the ignition switch.

duplicated in the next stretch of cable, and signals could be sent for unlimited distances without loss of strength.

This principle is still important today. A relay is a device that enables the current in one circuit to control the current in another. The second current may be large and therefore dangerous, while the first one is small and safe to operate, as when a truck driver brings an engine to life with a powerful current from the battery, controlled by a weak current that is switched on with the turn of the ignition key.

ELECTRICITY IN THE CAR

Apart from the starter relay and other relays, the modern car is packed with electrical devices in which magnetism plays a key role. Many devices are actually small motors, and they are discussed in detail later. There are also a variety of magnetic sensors. One detects the position of the throttle (in cars that have cruise control, which keeps a constant throttle setting without foot pressure for freeway driving). Another sensor detects the position of the steering wheel in cars with power steering, so that the amount of power that is delivered to help turn the wheel can be controlled precisely.

ELECTROMAGNETISM AND SOUND

Both in the car and outside it magnetism is essential to sound reproduction. Relatively weak electric currents, varying in strength many thousands of times per second, drive loudspeakers in a radio, CD player, or TV set. The pattern of the current—the audio signal—is a copy of the pattern of loudness of the voices, music, or other sounds that the current might be representing.

This varying current is passed through a solenoid called the voice coil, attached to the center of a paper or plastic cone. The coil is in the field of a strong permanent magnet that may take the form of, for example, a ring surrounding the coil. The varying current gives rise to a constantly fluctuating magnetic field generated by the coil, and the coil is pulled by the permanent magnet at a strength that depends on the current. The coil therefore vibrates, together with the cone that is attached to it. The vibrating cone disturbs the air, setting up sound waves that are exact copies of the original ones.

A microphone originally produces the electric current that carries the audio signal. In the most important types of microphone once again it is electromagnetism that plays a key role. The vibrations of sounds that strike the microphone cause a light plastic diaphragm to vibrate. Attached to the diaphragm is a metal ribbon or coil in the field of a permanent magnet.

As the metal vibrates in the field, the effect is the same as if the magnet were being moved while the metal remained still: a voltage is induced in the metal. This creates the small audio current.

The development of new types of electromagnetic microphones and

Each of these speakers contains a strong permanent magnet and a coil acting as an electromagnet. The interaction between them makes the speakers' cones (the dark disks) vibrate and generate sound.

loudspeakers in the years after World War I was an important advance in sound recording and broadcasting.

The first sound-recording machines had speaking tubes for microphones and large horns to amplify the faint sounds produced by the needle as it was dragged along the groove of a recording disk or cylinder. Electronic reproduction of sound proved to be more accurate, making possible a greater range of frequencies and greater volume when required.

Electromagnetism was used in a different way to revolutionize a musical instrument. Magnetic detectors called pickups were added to the steel-stringed guitar so that the vibrations of the strings were turned directly into electrical signals. They could be amplified (made stronger) or altered in various ways and then fed into a loudspeaker. This made the guitar into a powerful instrument that could accompany dance orchestras and jazz bands. Then, in the early days of rock and roll, it became a solo instrument. A wide repertoire of electronic effects was added, enabling the electric guitar to become the dominant instrument in pop and rock music.

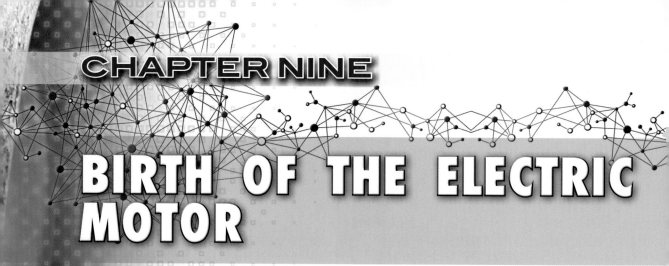

CHAPTER NINE

BIRTH OF THE ELECTRIC MOTOR

Magnetic fields produced by permanent magnets or electric currents can move current-carrying wires. Early researchers studied this effect and designed the first electric motors. Their laboratory toys grew into the workhorses of modern industry.

After Oersted's groundbreaking discovery of 1819, the British physicist Michael Faraday made the most thorough experimental investigation of the interactions between electricity and magnetism. The French physicist André Ampère had found that not only did current-carrying wires produce magnetic fields, they also experienced forces when

The great experimenter Michael Faraday made numerous discoveries in electricity.

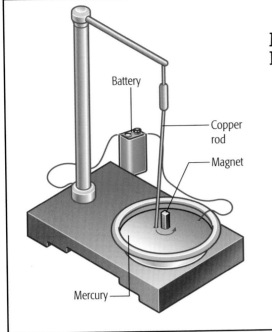

Battery

Copper
rod

Magnet

Mercury

MOTOR EFFECT DEMONSTRATION

When current flows through the copper rod dipping in the mercury, the rod revolves around the magnet.

they were placed in magnetic fields, making them seem even more similar to magnets.

Faraday announced his "left-hand motor rule" as a reminder of how these forces acted. Imagine that the thumb, first finger, and second finger of your left hand are extended at right angles to one another:

- if the first finger represents the direction of the field
- and the second finger represents the direction of the current
- then the thumb represents the direction of movement of the current-carrying wire.

(As always in this book, the direction of the current is taken to be the direction of flow of positive charge, the opposite of the direction of flow of the negatively charged electrons.)

THE MOTOR EFFECT

Faraday set up a very striking demonstration of the effect of the interaction between current and magnetism. He let a current flow through a freely suspended copper rod that was dipping in a pool of the liquid metal mercury (a good conductor). When a bar magnet was placed upright near the rod, the rod started to revolve around the magnet and kept revolving for as long as the current flowed. Because the current was roughly vertical and the magnetic field lines went

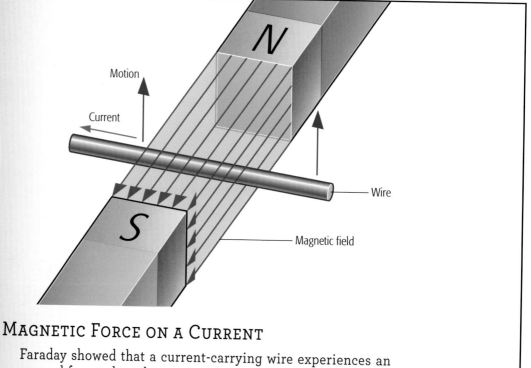

Motion

Current

Wire

Magnetic field

MAGNETIC FORCE ON A CURRENT

Faraday showed that a current-carrying wire experiences an upward force when the current and magnetic field are in the directions shown here.

to and from the magnet, there was a force on the rod at right angles to both of them—that is, around the circumference of a circle.

If a current is passed through a coil in a magnetic field, the two sides of the coil experience forces in opposite directions (because the current flows in opposite directions on the two sides of the coil). This creates a torque, or twisting force, on the coil (except when it is exactly at right angles to the field lines, when the forces tend to stretch or squeeze the coil, but not turn it). The more turns the coil has, the stronger the current, and the stronger the magnetic field, the stronger the force on it. This was to be the basis of the powerful electric motors of today.

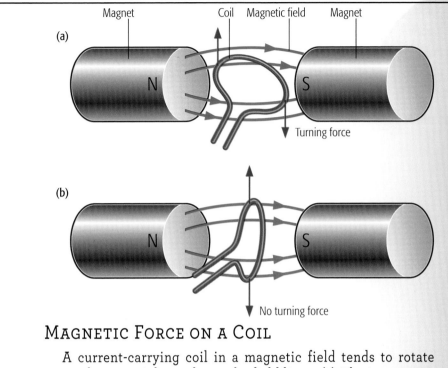

MAGNETIC FORCE ON A COIL

A current-carrying coil in a magnetic field tends to rotate until it is at right angles to the field lines. (a) The interaction between the magnetic field and the current causes the coil to turn. (b) When the coil is at right angles to the field, there is no turning force.

Today's electric cars use electric motors and electrical power stored in batteries.

CHAPTER TEN

TYPES OF MOTORS

Our civilization would collapse were it not for electric motors. There are many designs, each intended to do a particular job, from small motors in electric clocks to large winding motors for a skyscraper's elevators. They depend on ingenious engineering that exploits the intimate connection between electricity and magnetism.

The simple rotating coil shown in the previous chapter has to be made considerably more complicated to turn it into an electric motor. Yet the basic principle remains the same in all motors: an electric current moving through a magnetic field experiences a force at right angles to itself and to the field. The force can be turned into movement, and

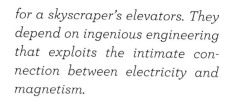

A powerful electric motor is needed to drive the lifting cable of a crane.

the movement can be made to do useful work such as moving a vehicle, or raising a weight, or opening a door.

DC MOTORS

Direct current (DC) is a steady current that does not vary with time. In the simplest sort of electric motor direct current is passed through a coil of many turns that is free to rotate in the field of a permanent magnet. In the upper illustration on the right, current flowing away from you experiences an upward force. With the coil in the position shown, the torque is therefore clockwise. When the plane of the coil is parallel to the field, like this, the torque (twisting force) on the coil is at its maximum.

When the coil has turned through 90 degrees from this position, there is no torque on it, but its momentum carries it past this point. If the flow of current were not altered, the torque on the coil would now be counterclockwise, tending to slow down the rotation. To prevent this, the current is reversed when the coil is at 90 degrees to the field.

The current is supplied through a commutator—a ring or cylinder split into two parts,

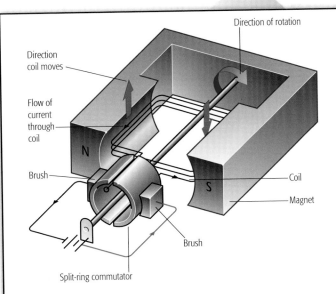

DC MOTOR

The magnetic field forces the current-carrying coil to rotate. Attached to the coil is the split-ring commutator, which reverses the current at every half-turn.

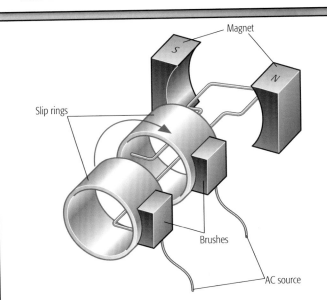

AC MOTOR

The direction of the current reverses continually, ensuring that the coil always experiences a turning force in the same direction.

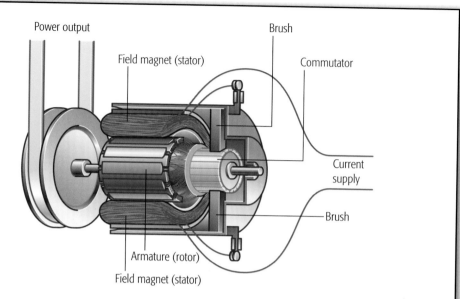

Power output

Field magnet (stator)

Brush

Commutator

Current supply

Brush

Armature (rotor)

Field magnet (stator)

PRACTICAL DC MOTOR

The magnetic field is provided not by a permanent magnet but by current passing through field magnet windings. The commutator has many segments, corresponding to the number of field magnet coils in the armature.

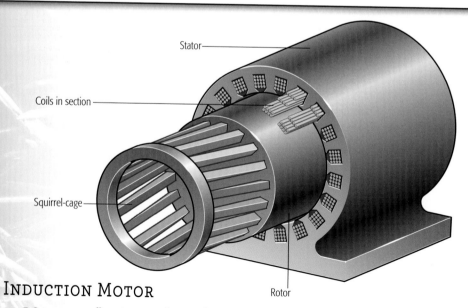

Stator

Coils in section

Squirrel-cage

Rotor

INDUCTION MOTOR

AC current flowing in the coils of the stator (the outer assembly) generates a rotating magnetic field that drags the rotor around.

each part touching one brush, or contact. As the coil turns to the 90-degree position, each half of the commutator comes into contact with the other brush, reversing the direction of flow into the coil. So the coil gets an increasing twist in the same direction as it turns through the next 90 degrees. When it has turned to the point where it is once again at right angles to the field, the current is again reversed.

AC MOTORS

An AC motor can in principle be simpler than this, as in the diagram on page 55. Because alternating current reverses itself periodically (the electricity supply goes through 60 cycles per second in the United States), there is no need for a commutator if the coil revolves at this rate. Such a motor will adjust its rate automatically to the frequency of the supplied current.

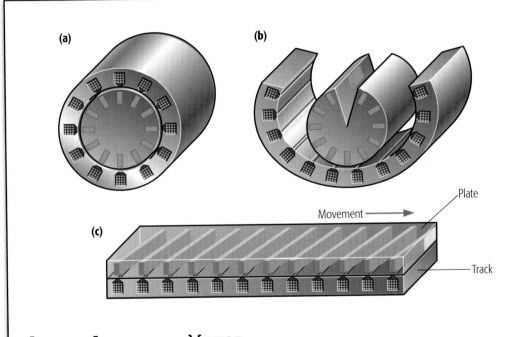

LINEAR INDUCTION MOTOR

If an induction motor (a) were imagined to be "unrolled" (b), it would form a linear induction motor (c). Traveling magnetic fields in the track pull the metal plate along.

Induction motors are used in ceiling fans. Semiconductors allow the motor to rotate the fan at variable speeds.

However, all practical motors have to be more complicated than these examples. The magnetic field is likely to be supplied by electromagnets rather than a permanent magnet.

The power supply to the motor sends some current through coils called field magnets around the outside of the motor in an assembly called the stator. There can be many rotating coils, making up an assembly called the rotor. It is supplied with current through a commutator divided into a corresponding number of segments, so that at any moment current flows into the coil that is in the plane of the field and so produces the maximum torque.

INDUCTION MOTORS

The most common type of AC motor is the induction motor, which works on a different principle from the one described above. In an induction motor AC current is passed through field coils in a stator, one coil after another, so that viewed from one end, the direction of the magnetic field rotates. Housed within the stator is a structure called a squirrel-cage, which consists of bars of iron or other soft magnetic metal. The revolving field in the stator induces a magnetic field in the squirrel-cage (hence the name "induction motor"). The squirrel-cage moves around with the field. (The speedometer illustrated on page 26 works on a similar principle, but with a revolving permanent magnet.)

Modern homes are full of machines and devices that utilize electric motors. These devices make many aspects of daily life much different than it was 100 years ago.

LINEAR INDUCTION MOTORS

A similar principle can be used in motors that move objects in straight lines. In the linear induction motor field coils are arranged along a track. A pulse of current passes through successive coils in turn, sending a wave of magnetism along the track.

A flat plate of suitable metal laid on or alongside the track has magnetism induced in it and moves along with the wave. Linear induction motors are widely used for sliding doors and in some other machines, such as the shuttles of looms, where straight-line motion is required.

POWERING THE WORLD

In industrialized countries electric motors are present everywhere, running countless details of our lives where we might not suspect their presence. A car

Sliding doors, often used at grocery stores, hospital emergency rooms, and many other places, are an example of a linear induction motor in action.

Assembly lines, like the one assembling automobiles seen here, are powered by electric motors. When the cars are ready to drive, they will be powered by electric motors, too.

is a good place to find them. Small electric motors drive windshield wipers and washers, electric windows, sunroofs, centrally controlled door locks—and even adjustable rear-view mirrors, seats, and the extending radio antenna.

Domestic machines, including dishwashers, washing machines, food-blenders, juicers, power drills, and vacuum cleaners, all rely on electric motors. Even a desktop computer has motors in it to power its disk drives and cooling fan. In factories, assembly lines, cranes, drills, lathes, and a host of other machines are driven by electric motors. And every one of these electric motors relies on magnetism.

CHAPTER ELEVEN

ELECTRIC MOTORS EVERYWHERE

The world generates most of its energy from coal, oil, gas, and nuclear fuel. A large fraction of this energy is converted into electricity and put to work by means of electric motors, which are everywhere around us.

Industrialization began in the 18th century with water power, applied in cotton mills and other factories. It was followed by steam power. The development of the electric motor in the 19th century carried industrialization into a new phase and made possible the development of many new devices. By 1850 experimental electric motors were powering boats and railroad locomotives.

Today the sorts of jobs that electric motors have to do are very diverse. Some have to move large weights through large distances, such as those that raise large passenger elevators in tall office buildings. Others

Miners are carried to underground tunnels by elevators. They are raised and lowered by cables running over the pulley wheels at the top of the tower and pulled by the motor at the foot of the tower.

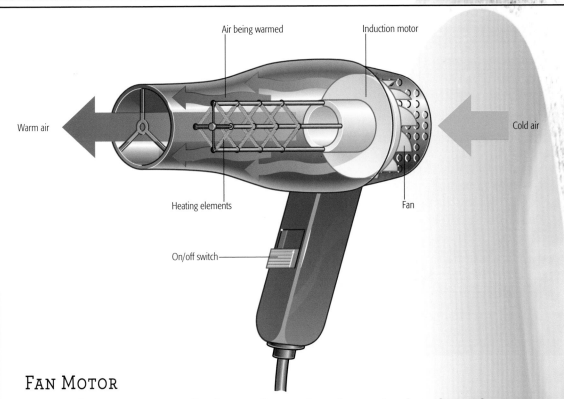

Air being warmed

Induction motor

Warm air

Cold air

Heating elements

Fan

On/off switch

FAN MOTOR

An induction motor usually drives a fan, such as the one in a hair-drier. Alternating current is supplied to field coils that produce a rotating magnetic field. The rotating field turns an aluminum rotor on which the fan is mounted. There may be a speed control that alters the rate of rotation of the field and therefore of the fan.

turn the hands on a watch. Some have to provide a smooth movement, such as the motors operating sliding doors; while with others, such as those in garbage-disposal units, the power that can be developed is more important. Some must be very small, like those that must fit into a personal CD player. With electric motors used in industry, size may be limited by the cost of large motors.

GOING UP!

The passenger elevator was made possible by the advent of the electric motor. A steam-operated passenger elevator had gone into service in a New York City department store in 1857. Though steam-operated and hydraulic elevators were successful, electrically powered ones took their place in the late 1880s. They

Many modern city skylines are dominated by skyscrapers. Skyscrapers were made practical by the advent of the electric motor and the elevator.

were cleaner, quieter, more powerful, and more flexible, and types of motor were soon introduced that allowed the cars to be operated at a wide range of speeds without complicated gearing. The motors driving the fastest modern elevators can move them at 45 kph (28 mph).

Tall modern buildings need so many elevators that designers are trying to get them to occupy smaller amounts of space. One way that is being explored is to take the motors away from the winding gear at the top of the shaft and replace them with flat linear induction motors built into the elevator car.

VARIATIONS AND ADJUSTMENTS

There are countless variations in the design of electric motors to deal with the differing circumstances in which they are used. There may be special adjustments to help them start slowly or prevent them from starting too quickly and violently.

Current going to a motor's stator flows through the field coils, creating a magnetic field directed across the stator. In the simplest type of motor, called a two-pole motor, this field constantly reverses through 180 degrees because the supply is AC and so reverses continually. The rotor has its own magnetic field, which is produced by a permanent magnet or by current. It swings around repeatedly, "trying" to bring its own north pole close to the south pole of the stator field, but never succeeding because the stator field is constantly switching. This kind of motor can be slow to get started. If, when the motor is switched on, the rotor field happens to be lined up with the stator field, then when the stator field flips the rotor does not get a twist to one side or the other. Once the rotor is moving there is no problem—its own momentum carries it past this neutral position. Also, it can rotate equally well in either direction, so it has to be given an initial nudge in the right direction. Such a motor comes with an additional field coil and circuits that create an extra field when the device is started; but once the motor is up to speed, they are disconnected automatically.

Often a motor has more than two poles—that is, more than one pair of field coils. As explained in the previous chapter, current is sent to these pairs in succession to create a magnetic field

Escalators are another way to move from one level of a building to another. A pair of chains loop around a pair of gears, which are turned by an electric motor.

that rotates, as seen from one end of the motor. This kind of motor generally has no startup problem.

In some kinds of motor there is a different kind of problem on starting. The motor is liable to start moving violently if full voltage is applied to it on switch-on. This would not do in streetcars and elevators, say, which must not jolt violently. Additional circuits are built into motors for such applications, which limit the field that is developed in the motor's rotor immediately after switch-on and are disconnected later.

STEADY AND SYNCHRONOUS

There are many applications in which it is important for the motor to turn at a steady speed. One is any kind of sound recording and playback, whether in a traditional phonograph turntable, a CD drive, or a tape drive. Another is in clocks and watches (the analog sort, which have hands). The AC supply from the power company is an ideal "pacemaker" for a motor because it is delivered at a constant frequency (60 cycles a second in the United States). If it is supplied to the

Electric streetcars and trams, such as the one seen here in Portugal, must be able to start and stop at slower speeds.

stator of a motor, it will generate a field rotating 60 times a second. If the rotor is equipped with a permanent magnet, or with an electromagnet supplied by a fixed-strength direct current, the rotor will follow the rotating field at the same rate. Such a motor is called "synchronous."

Motors used in watches and other portable devices clearly have to be very small.

In the 1970s it became possible to miniaturize components to the point where a motor could be compact yet powerful enough to power a personal tape-player, and the Sony Corporation marketed the Walkman, which later spawned a host of other personal audio devices.

To keep accurate time, the motors in clocks and wristwatches much move at a steady speed.

CHAPTER TWELVE

ELECTROMAGNETISM ON THE MOVE

Noise and atmospheric pollution, the bane of modern city life, are caused mostly by motor vehicles. For decades visionaries have dreamed of silent, clean electric cars and trucks. Many companies are working to develop electric vehicles in which the clean, quiet forces of electromagnetism will be put to work to move people and freight.

A few types of battery-operated vehicle, such as forklift trucks in factories, are used today. In the future there may be more commuter vehicles that get their power wholly from batteries. They would be recharged overnight or perhaps changed when low at the equivalent of a filling

Magnetic-levitation rail vehicles, such as this one in Shanghai, China, are held a few millimeters off the track by electromagnets that curve beneath the track and are attracted up toward it.

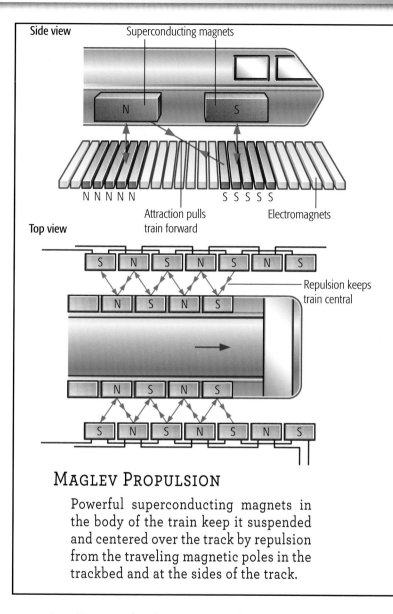

Side view

Superconducting magnets

N

S

N N N N

S S S S

Attraction pulls
train forward

Electromagnets

Top view

S N S N S N S

N S N S

Repulsion keeps
train central

N S N S

S N S N S N S

MAGLEV PROPULSION

Powerful superconducting magnets in
the body of the train keep it suspended
and centered over the track by repulsion
from the traveling magnetic poles in the
trackbed and at the sides of the track.

be teamed with bat-
teries. The flywheels
would provide bursts
of power when needed
for acceleration; the
batteries would pro-
vide steady low power
for cruising. The fly-
wheels would have to
be made of supertough
materials because they
would spin at 100,000
revolutions per second,
which would tear apart
flywheels made from
ordinary materials. To
reduce friction so that
the flywheel did not
lose energy, it would be
supported on magnetic
bearings, held away
from physical con-
tact with its container
by magnetic fields.
The flywheel would
need to be revved up
from time to time to
replace the energy
used on journeys.
Energy could also be
stored in "ultracapaci-
tors," devices that store
large quantities of electricity. Again, they
would most likely be teamed with batteries in hybrid systems.

Today, hybrid systems in which
energy storage are combined with gaso-
line engines to drive electric motors are
becoming more and more popular. The
gas engines provide only the relatively

station. Present-day batteries are heavy
and store relatively little energy. A battery-operated car of today is able to travel
only about 150 km (90 miles) before it
needs to be recharged.

But in the future the battery may
be combined with, or even replaced
by, other devices already in operation
experimentally. Ultrafast flywheels could

low power needed for steady cruising. These hybrid engines are far more economical and clean than the more powerful engines typical in other vehicles powered only by gas.

BRAKING ENERGY

A feature of all electrical propulsion systems is that some of the energy that is normally wasted in braking can be stored and reused. Instead of conventional brakes, magnets attached to a vehicle's wheels induce electric currents in a circuit and charge up a battery, or store the energy some other way, while at the same time the vehicle is slowed. Later the stored energy can be used to boost the vehicle's speed.

ELECTRIC STREETCARS

There are many vehicles in the world today that use electrical energy, not from self-contained sources on the vehicle but from the public supply, via rails and overhead lines. Streetcars supplied from overhead electrical lines were popular in many cities in the early 20th century and today are enjoying a revival. They do not have the freedom of movement of gasoline-fueled buses, but are cheaper to run and are less polluting.

THE FRENCH TGV

French high-speed trains are powered from overhead lines and have set speed records of over 515 kph (320 mph). Ninety percent of the braking on the newest TGVs is provided by "dynamic" (regenerative) brakes, which reclaim energy for reuse.

ELECTRICITY BY RAIL

The major use for electrical vehicle propulsion today is for railroads. Although the first subway trains, in the late 19th century, were powered by steam, electricity was adopted as soon as it became available because steam and smoke were unpleasant and even dangerous in the confines of subway tunnels. Electricity is nearly always preferred for the light railways or rapid-transit systems being built in increasing numbers of cities. And it is also the preferred system of powering long-distance trains all over Europe. However, even diesel trains are usually better described as diesel-electric, because most use their diesel engines to generate the electricity that turns the wheels.

Since 1981 France has had a network of high-speed rail services operated by electric trains called TGVs (for Train à Grande Vitesse—High-Speed Train). Each train is propelled by two power cars, one at each end. One of them collects power from

Dynamic brakes

overhead lines by an assembly called a pantograph. There are different ones for lower and higher voltages. Part of the power is sent along cables to the other power car. Each motor delivers 1,100 kilowatts. The latest TGVs operate at 360 kph (225 mph), and in the future they may exceed 400 kph (250 mph) in normal service.

MAGNETIC LEVITATION

Still faster speeds will be feasible if trains are separated from the track altogether. That can be done by setting up powerful magnetic fields in the body of the train and in the track that repel each other, a process called magnetic levitation, or maglev. Maglev trains can be supported by repulsion, with the whole train and its magnets above the track, or by attraction, with "wings" mounted

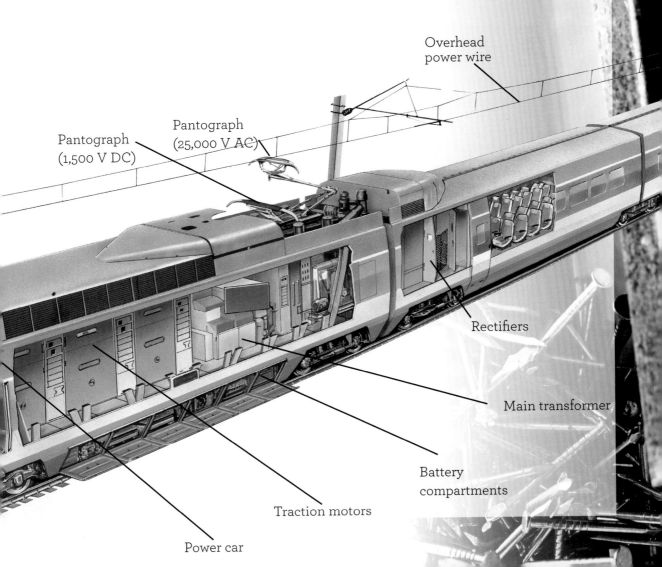

Overhead power wire

Pantograph (1,500 V DC)

Pantograph (25,000 V AC)

Rectifiers

Main transformer

Battery compartments

Traction motors

Power car

on the bottom of the train to carry its magnets. They curl around under the track and are lifted up toward it. Maglev trains are economical because there is almost no resistance between the train and the track. Also, if they use super-conducting magnets, in which the magnet has been cooled to such a temperature that it has no electrical resistance, then very little energy is lost in maintaining the field. Superconducting maglev trains could become the most advanced way of harnessing magnetism to meet our transport needs.

Most subway systems are powered by overhead wires or an electrified third rail. When using a third rail, a wheel, brush, or sliding show carries electricity from the rail to the motor of the train.

CHAPTER THIRTEEN

BIOGRAPHY: JOSEPH HENRY

Joseph Henry was one of the United States' greatest scientists. He is often referred to as the successor to Benjamin Franklin. Henry was a man of many interests and achievements. He made many enormous contributions to science. One of his best known contributions was the discovery of electromagnetic phenomenon of self-inductance.

Joseph Henry was born on December 17th, 1797, in Albany, New York. His parents, who were named Ann and William, emigrated from Scotland to New York in 1775. Henry's father worked as a laborer and died when Henry was young. Henry's family was very poor and with the death of his father, his mother was unable to support him so he was sent to live with his grandmother in Galway, New York. He began attending a public school in Galway, which would much later be renamed the Joseph Henry Elementary School after him. As a boy, Henry had no particular interest in science. He was very interested in theater and thought of becoming a professional actor. He also loved to read. When he was 13, he was

Joseph Henry made advances in the way we communicate over distances, use electricity, and predict the weather.

KEY DATES

1797	Born in Albany, New York
1819	Enrolls at the Albany Academy
1820	Marries Harriet Alexander
1824	Appointed assistant engineer
1826	Becomes Professor of Mathematics and Natural Philosophy at the Albany Academy
1827	Begins experiments with electromagnetics
1832	Accepts position as professor at the College of New Jersey (Princeton)
1846	Named first Secretary of the Smithsonian
1847	Moves to Washington, D.C.
1863	Founds National Academy of Science
1877	Dies at 80 years old in Washington, D.C.

apprenticed to a watchmaker. Henry was raised a Presbyterian and remained very religious throughout his life.

It wasn't until he was sixteen years old that Henry developed an interest in science. When he was sixteen he read *Popular Lectures on Experimental Philosophy, Astronomy, and Chemistry.* Henry became enthralled with science and abandoned his dream of becoming an actor.

COLLEGE YEARS

In 1819, with the encouragement of friends, Joseph Henry enrolled in the Albany Academy. Albany Academy was the equivalent of a modern day college. Henry was given free tuition, but he was still very poor. To support himself, he worked as a teacher and a private tutor, specializing in mathematics. While at the Academy, in 1820, Henry married his cousin Harriet Alexander. They went on to have four children, named William, Caroline, Helen, and Mary.

Henry intended to go into medicine. However, that desire was put on hold, in 1824, when he was appointed to an assistant engineer position for the survey of the state road. The road was to run between Lake Erie and the Hudson River, a distance of 300 miles. This work inspired an interest in engineering in Henry.

Henry did very well at the Albany Academy. So well, in fact, that he was often called upon to help his teachers instruct.

Joseph Henry's explorations with electromagnetism were crucial to the later development of the telegraph, which allowed messages to be sent over great distances.

In 1826, he was appointed Professor of Mathematics and Natural Philosophy at the Academy. While in that position, Henry developed an interest in electromagnetism. Henry became interested in the field after reading about the experiments done by European scientists. Electromagnetism is the creation of a magnetic field from the movement of electric currents.

WORK WITH ELECTROMAGNETS

Henry began his exploration of electromagnetism out of a desire to help his students. In 1827, Henry published a paper on electromagnetism in which he lamented the difficulty in introducing his students to electromagnetism. Electromagnets at the time were expensive, delicate, and awkward. In the paper, Henry described improvements on other

ALEXANDER GRAHAM BELL

Alexander Graham Bell is best known as the inventor of the telephone. Bell's mother and wife were deaf, which led him to his research on hearing, speech, and hearing devices. This research and interest in the field led to the invention of the telephone in 1875.

scientists' electromagnets. Though his improvements did not constitute a new discovery, they did improve on electromagnets as educational tools and set Henry on his path toward invention.

Next, Henry went about creating an even stronger electromagnet. The English scientist William Sturgeon made the first electromagnets in 1824. He had loosely coiled uninsulated copper wire around a horseshoe shaped piece of iron. When a current was passed through the iron it became magnetized. This was an amazing discovery, but the magnet created by Sturgeon was quite weak. Henry created a stronger magnet by insulating the wire with silk thread. This allowed for a tighter coil. Henry's electromagnet had 400 tight turns and used 35 feet of wire. Sturgeon's magnet, on the other hand, had only 18 turns. At the time, Henry's electromagnet was the strongest in existence.

Henry's distinguished between "quantity" circuits and "intensity" circuits. "Quantity" circuits had a high amperage, while "intensity" circuits had a high voltage. With his understanding of electrical circuits, Henry was able to build an electromagnet that could hold up to 750 pounds of iron! Despite its huge

amount of power, the electromagnet was not extremely expensive, making it an excellent tool for teaching.

Using his electromagnets, Henry also discovered the concept of self-inductance. He did this by conducting an experiment where he sent a current through a wire in the second story of a building. The current induced currents in a similar wire in the basement.

THE INFLUENCE OF HENRY'S ELECTROMAGNET

Henry's discoveries were precursors to both the invention of the telegraph and the electric motor. In 1830, Henry demonstrated the potential of using electromagnets for long distance communication. He sent an electric current over 1 mile of wire to activate an electromagnet which caused a bell to strike. This was the beginning of the telegraph. Other scientists went on to make the telegraph a useful tool.

Henry's work is also credited with bringing about the invention of the telephone. Alexander Graham Bell, the inventor of the telephone, said: "But for

Joseph Henry, I would never have gone ahead with the telephone."

THE ELECTRIC MOTOR

In 1831, Henry built one of the first machines to use electromagnetism for motion. It was an electromagnet on top of a pole, rocking back and forth. The rocking was caused by two leads on both ends of the magnet rocker touching one of two battery cells. This caused a change in polarity and a rocking motion. Henry's invention led to the invention of the first real electric motor in 1834. The first real electric motor was built by Thomas Davenport. Davenport used his motor to operate a small model of a car and train. This invention helped to bring on the development of streetcars.

PRINCETON PROFESSOR

In 1832, Henry accepted a position as a professor at the College of New Jersey, which later became known as Princeton. The position appealed to Henry not only because he loved to teach, but also because the College gave professors ample time to pursue their own research.

At the College of New Jersey, Henry taught natural philosophy, geology, and architecture. Though his specialty was in electromagnetism, Henry published papers on a variety of subjects including acoustics, astrophysics, and optics. Henry was a widely known and respected scientist in the United States and solidified this reputation with a European tour. He visited various science centers throughout Europe and created a network of scientific colleagues for himself.

THE SMITHSONIAN

In 1846, Henry became the first Secretary at the newly formed Smithsonian.

Joseph Henry taught at Princeton University between 1832 and 1846. He rigged a wire between his office in Philosophical Hall and his home on campus to send signals to his wife.

The decision to leave New Jersey for Washington, D.C., where the Smithsonian is located, was not an easy one. Henry and his family had made a home for themselves in Princeton. Henry's wife, Harriet, did not want to move. At the time, Washington, D.C., was known mostly for its heat, humidity, and poor sanitation. However, Henry was very committed to the idea of advancing American science, and working at the Smithsonian was an excellent opportunity to do so. Henry moved alone to Washington, D.C., ahead of his family in 1847.

The move south was a big adjustment. Henry and his family were largely private, modest people. But, with Henry's new job his family became part of Washington's elite. With his high profile job, Henry left much of his serious scientific research behind. He also no longer had time to teach. That does not mean that he stopped contributing to the scientific community, however.

In 1852, Henry was appointed to the United States Light-House Board. In that role, he chaired a committee responsible for testing oils, lamps, and other equipment. Henry also served his country during the Civil War. He was on a naval commission that helped develop new models for ships and weapons.

The Henry family remained in Washington, D.C., for the Civil War. The family was cut off from contact with their relatives in the north for much of the war.

The Smithsonian did not sustain any damage as a result of the war, but it was badly damaged in a large fire. Much of Henry's work was destroyed in the fire including scientific papers and correspondence. It was also around this time that Henry's son, William, died. In 1862, William contracted jaundice and succumbed to the illness within a few days.

In 1863, Henry helped to found the National Academy of Sciences. The Academy advised the federal government on scientific questions. In 1868, he became the director of the Academy and remained in that position until his death.

Joseph Henry's advances in storm and weather tracking led to the development of modern meteorological studies.

SMITHSONIAN

Today, the Smithsonian Institute is the world's largest museum and research complex. It is made up of 19 museums, 9 research centers, and the National Zoo. The Smithsonian's holdings include 137 million items, and it is often called the "nation's attic."

METEOROLOGY

Henry was a man of many interests. Though he specialized in electromagnetism, he also had an intense interest in meteorology. This interest began at the Albany Academy where Henry would compile reports of statewide meteorological observations for the University of the State of New York. While at the College of New Jersey, Henry researched storm patterns, atmospheric physics, and lightning.

In fact, when Henry first started at the Smithsonian one of his main priorities was to establish a meteorological program. By 1849, Henry had 150 volunteer weather observers. Over the next 10 years, that number rose to 600 volunteers around the United States and in Canada, Mexico, and the Caribbean. Compiling all of the observations took time. In 1861, Henry published the first of a two-volume compilation.

Henry also saw the potential of the telegraph as a storm-warning tool. Since storms generally move west to east, Henry believed that the telegraph could be used to warn of storms advancing to the east. Henry made arrangements with a number of telegraph companies to allow free transmissions of local weather to the Smithsonian. The information gathered from the telegraphs allowed Henry to create a daily weather map. Henry put the map up for public display in the Smithsonian. An assistant would put up colored discs throughout the map of the country. Each color represented a different type of weather.

The weather map was so popular among tourists that Henry began sharing his weather information with various newspapers, thus creating the first weather pages. The map also allowed for the beginning of weather forecasting. With the knowledge of the weather in one city, Henry could make an educated guess of what the weather would be in the next city over.

This statue of Joseph Henry stands outside the Smithsonian in Washington, D.C.

Much of Henry's meteorological work was disrupted by the Civil War. After the war. Henry called on the federal government to create a weather bureau for issuing storm warnings and making other weather predictions. This bureau would later become known as the National Weather Service.

LATER YEARS AND LEGACY

Henry was an avid researcher with an invested interested in advancing science in America. He devoted much of his time to encouraging scientific research and discovery. Henry had little interest in the commercial applications of his discoveries, leaving that to other scientists. He was extremely well respected and quite famous during his lifetime. Henry continues to be an inspiration to scientists and educators today.

Beyond his accomplishments as an inventor and researcher, he was also an excellent teacher. He was beloved by his students at both the Albany Academy and at Princeton. It was his love of teaching that led to his initial research into the electromagnet. Henry was the vice president of the Friends of Public Education and later became the president of the American Association for the Advancement of Education.

In December 1877 Henry suffered an attack that was initially diagnosed as stroke but was later discovered to be caused by a kidney condition known as Bright's Disease. Henry died five months later at 80 years old. Henry's funeral was compared to Abraham Lincoln's by the press, based on its size and prestigious guests. In 1883, a statue of Joseph Henry was erected at the National Mall in Washington, D.C., in front of the Smithsonian. In 1893, the standard electrical unit for inductive resistance was named the "henry" after Joseph Henry.

SCIENTIFIC BACKGROUND

1724 Benjamin Franklin
discovers positive and
negative charges.

1769 Nicolas-Joseph Cugnot
invents the steam-powered
tricycle.

1780 Luigi Galvani discovers
electricity from two different
metals causes a frog's legs
to twitch.

1817 William Murdoch invents compressed air powered doorbell

1818 Baron Karl von Drais invents the dandy horse, the precursor to the bicycle

1824 William Sturgeon builds the first electromagnets

1826 Nicéphore Niépce makes the first permanent photograph using a camera obscura

1832 Samuel Morse develops the telegraph

1834 Thomas Davenport constructs first DC electric motor

1866 First successful transatlantic telegraph is sent

1875 Alexander Graham Bell develops the acoustic telegraph, the precursor to the telephone

1886 Carl Benz creates first modern automobile, the Benz Patent-Motorwagen

1895 Gugliemo Marconi sends messages via radio signals

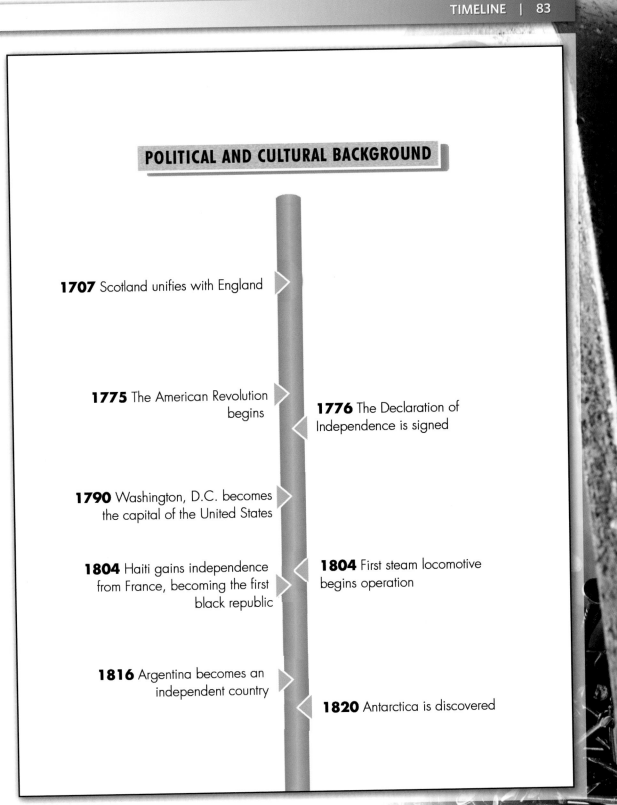

POLITICAL AND CULTURAL BACKGROUND

1707 Scotland unifies with England

1775 The American Revolution begins

1776 The Declaration of Independence is signed

1790 Washington, D.C. becomes the capital of the United States

1804 Haiti gains independence from France, becoming the first black republic

1804 First steam locomotive begins operation

1816 Argentina becomes an independent country

1820 Antarctica is discovered

1845 The Irish potato famine, which devastes Ireland, begins

1846 The Smithsonian is founded

1859 Construction begins on the Suez Canal

1861 The American Civil War, fought between the Union and the Confederacy, begins

1861 Abraham Lincoln is elected president of the United States

1867 United States purchases Alaska from Russia

1865 Abraham Lincoln is assissinated

AC See *alternating current*.

AC motor An electric motor that is operated by alternating current.

alternating current (AC) Electric current that flows first in one direction, then in the other, alternating many times each second. AC is used for domestic electricity supply and many other electrical applications.

ampere (A) The SI unit of electric current. A current of 1 ampere (often abbreviated to "amp") is equal to a flow of 1 coulomb of charge per second.

atom The smallest part of a chemical element that can exist on its own. It has a central nucleus, surrounded by electrons.

aurora Glowing lights in the atmosphere, seen usually at high latitudes, caused by charged particles from the Sun that are trapped temporarily in the from Earth's radiation belts and then "spill over" into the atmosphere.

bar magnet A permanent magnet that is bar-shaped, having a magnetic pole at each end. See also *horseshoe magnet*.

brush A fixed electrical contact, made of carbon or metal, that presses against a moving part in a machine to maintain electrical contact.

commutator Part of a generator or motor that converts alternating current or voltage into direct current or voltage.

coil A spiral of wire through which current flows. The magnetic fields of the current in the different turns of the coil add together to make a large magnetic field. The coil is then an electromagnet, with a field resembling that of a bar magnet.

core A piece of iron placed in a coil to make it a more powerful electromagnet. When current flows in the coil, generating a magnetic field, the core becomes strongly magnetized.

coulomb (C) The SI unit of electric charge. It is equal to the charge carried by 6.24 billion billion electrons.

current A flow of electric charge. The current from the domestic electricity supply, from generators, and from batteries consists of a flow of electrons.

DC See *direct current*.

DC motor An electric motor that is operated by direct current.

declination The angle between the direction of magnetic north and true north.

deviation The angle between the direction of magnetic north and the direction in which a magnetic compass needle actually points, owing to the attraction of nearby metal.

diamagnetic material A material that in a magnetic field becomes weakly magnetized in the opposite direction from the field. The magnetization decreases to zero when the material is removed from the field. Most materials are diamagnetic. See also *ferromagnetic material; paramagnetic material*.

dip The angle between the direction in which a magnetic compass needle points and the horizontal.

direct current (DC) Electric current that flows in one direction all the time, though it may vary in strength.

domain A small region in a magnetic material in which the magnetic fields of individual atoms all point in the same direction, making the domain into a single small magnet. In the unmagnetized material fields of different domains point in different directions, canceling one another out.

dynamo An electrical generator, especially one that produces direct current.

electromagnet A device that develops a magnetic field when electric current is passed through it. It consists of a coil with a core.

electromagnetic induction Generation of a voltage caused by changes in a magnetic field or by the movement of an electrical conductor through a magnetic field.

electromagnetic radiation Waves of visible light, ultraviolet and infrared radiation, microwaves, and radio waves. They all consist of electric and magnetic fields oscillating at different rates.

electromagnetism The interlinked phenomena of electricity and magnetism. Every electric current generates a magnetic field, while changes in a magnetic field can cause a current to flow.

electron A subatomic particle that carries a negative charge. Most electric currents consist of electrons in motion.

ferromagnetic material A metal such as iron that can become strongly magnetized when it is placed in a magnetic field, and which retains its magnetism when the field is removed. See also *diamagnetic material; domain; paramagnetic material.*

field The pattern of magnetic, electric, gravitational, or other influence around an object. See also *line of force.*

force An influence that changes the shape, position, or movement of an object.

generator A machine that produces an electric current. It contains coils that are rotated in a magnetic field.

horseshoe magnet A permanent magnet that is bent into a horseshoe shape so that the two magnetic poles are close together, and their strengths combine. See also *bar magnet.*

induction motor An electric motor in which a moving magnetic field induces (generates) current in another component, which moves to follow the field. The moving part may revolve or move in a straight line. See also *linear induction motor.*

left–hand motor rule When the directions of a magnetic field and electric current are represented by the first and second fingers respectively of the left hand, the direction of motion of the current-carrying conductor is indicated by the thumb when all three digits are extended at right angles to one another. See also *electromagnetic induction; right-hand dynamo rule.*

line of force An imaginary line whose direction at any point in a field shows the direction of the field at that point.

linear induction motor An induction motor that produces straight-line motion, as, for example, in making a sliding door close and open.

lodestone A naturally magnetic iron ore, once used to make magnetic compasses.

maglev Abbreviation for magnetic levitation, the technology for keeping vehicles such as trains a few centimeters above the track on which they run by means of mutually repelling magnetic fields, to overcome friction.

magnetic compass A device in which a freely rotating magnetized needle indicates the direction of magnetic north.

magnetic disk A device for storing data, used mainly in computers, consisting of a disk coated with a magnetic material. At each point on the disk the magnetization of the material represents a single piece of data, either a 1 or a 0.

magnetic equator The imaginary circle around the Earth, approximately halfway between the planet's magnetic poles, where the Earth's magnetic field is horizontal.

magnetic lens An arrangement of electromagnets that can focus a beam of electrons or other charged particles, as in an electron microscope.

magnetic moment A measure of how strongly a magnet will be affected by a magnetic field. For a bar magnet it depends on the strength of each pole and the distance between them, while for an electromagnet it depends on the strength of the current and the number of coils.

magnetic north The direction in which a magnetic compass points (in the northern hemisphere). Except in the polar regions, this direction is close enough to the true north–south line to be valuable to navigators.

magnetic resonance imaging (MRI) The technique of making pictures of the inside of, for example, the living human body. A person is placed in a strong magnetic field and bathed in radio waves. Hydrogen atoms in the body reveal themselves by "rebroadcasting" the waves.

magnetic tape A medium for storing data, consisting of a plastic tape coated with a magnetic material. At each point on the tape the magnetization of the material represents information.

magnetization The process of making an object or material into a magnet.

magnetosphere The region around the Earth or other celestial body in which its magnetic field is stronger than the field in surrounding space.

monopole An object with only one magnetic pole. No one has ever observed a monopole, though in theory it could exist.

motor A machine that converts energy, usually electrical energy, into motion.

MRI See *magnetic resonance imaging*.

paleomagnetism The magnetism found in ancient rocks, which gives information about changes in the Earth's crust going back millions of years into the past.

paramagnetic material A material that in a magnetic field itself becomes magnetized in the same direction as that of the field, though not strongly. It loses the magnetization when the external field is removed. See also *diamagnetic material; ferromagnetic material*.

permanent magnet A magnet that is not an electromagnet, and is made of a material such as iron or steel that keeps its magnetism even when no magnetic field is applied to it.

pole One of the two regions of a magnet where the strength of the field is greatest. Lines of force diverge (radiate out) from one pole and converge on the other. See also *monopole*.

radiation belts Regions around a planet, such as the Earth, or around a natural satellite (a moon) of a planet, in which charged particles from the Sun and space are trapped by the planet or satellite's magnetic field. See also *aurora*.

relay A device that is activated by changes in an electric current in a circuit, causing it to switch a second electric circuit on or off. Relays often incorporate electromagnets.

right-hand dynamo rule When the directions of a magnetic field and of movement of a current-carrying conductor are represented by the first finger and thumb respectively of the right hand, the direction of the current that is induced is indicated by the second finger, when all three digits are extended at right angles to one another. See also *electromagnetic induction; left-hand motor rule*.

rock magnetism The weak magnetism that most rocks have. It is like a "fossil" record of the Earth's magnetic field at the time the rocks were formed.

rotor In electromagnetic technology the rotating coil in a motor or generator. See also *stator*.

solenoid A current-carrying coil of wire. When a current flows through a solenoid, a magnetic field is developed in it. Often there is a moving iron core in the coil that moves when it is attracted by the magnetic field.

spin A property of some elementary particles, including electrons, which gives them each a tiny magnetic moment.

stator The stationary part of a motor or generator. See also *rotor*.

superconductivity The property of conducting electricity with no resistance at all. Some metals do this when cooled to a temperature close to absolute zero (-273.15°C/-459.67°F). New complex substances have been developed that superconduct at ever higher temperatures (though not yet as high as 0°C).

synchronous motor An electric motor in which the magnetic field rotates and the rotor moves around in time with it.

transformer A device that increases or decreases the voltage of alternating current.

Van Allen belts Another name for the Earth's radiation belts.

variation The change over time in the direction of magnetic north owing to movement of the Earth's magnetic poles.

American Meteorological Society
45 Beacon Street
Boston, MA 02108
617-227-2425
Web site: http://www.ametsoc.org
This organization promotes research
and sharing of information on the
atmosphere and related sciences.
The AMS publishes print and online
journals and sponsors several confer-
ences each year.

Electric Auto Association
323 Los Altos Drive
Aptos, CA 95003
831-688-8669
Web site: http://www.electricauto.org/
This organization, formed in 1967, seeks
to promote the advancement and
widespread use of electric vehicles.
The group shares information about
new developments in technology,
encourages experimentation in the
construction of new electric models,
and organizes exhibits and events to
inform the general public about the
benefits of electric vehicles.

European Organization for Nuclear
Research (CERN)
CH-1211 Geneva 23
Switzerland
+41 (0) 22 76 784 84
Web site: http://home.web.cern.ch/
CERN, established in 1954, is home to
the largest and most powerful parti-
cle accelerator in the world as well as
a laboratory that hosts 10,000

visiting scientists and engineers
from over 600 universities and
research facilities. Visitors may tour
the extensive laboratory and see
exhibits on such topics as the big
bang theory and how scientists use
particle accelerators to explore the
mysteries of the universe.

International Atomic Energy Agency
Vienna International Centre
P.O. Pox 100
1400 Vienna, Austria
(+43-1) 2600-0
Web site: http://www.iaea.org/
This group, part of the United Nations, is
the world's center of cooperation in
the field of nuclear physics. It was
organized in 1957 under the idea of
"atoms for peace," based in part on a
speech by US President Dwight D.
Eisenhower, with the goal of promot-
ing safe, secure, and peaceful nuclear
developments.

Mariner's Museum
100 Museum Drive
Newport News, VA 23606
757-596-2222
Web site: http://www.marinersmuseum.
org/
This museum focuses on the history of
our relationship with the ocean, from
early explorers to modern ships. The
collection includes many examples
of navigational tools bases on magnetic principles that allowed people
to navigate the seas.

Museum of the Moving Image
36-01 35th Avenue
Astoria, NY 11106
718-784-0077
Website: http://www.movingimage.us/
The Museum of the Moving Image cele-
brates the history, artistic vision, and
technology of film, television, and
digital media. The core exhibition
features over 1,400 artifacts related
the moving images, including early
examples of television sets that used
cathode ray tubes to create images.

National Weather Service
1325 East West Highway
Silver Spring, MD 20910
Web site: http://www.weather.gov
The division of the US government, part
of the National Oceanic and
Atmospheric Administration, provides weather, water, and climate
information, forecasts, and warnings.
Each year the service collects 76 billion observations and provides 1.5
million weather forecasts and 50,000
warnings about dangerous
conditions.

Smithsonian National Air and Space
Museum
Independence Avenue at 6th Street SW
Washington, DC 20560
202-633-2214
Web site: http://airandspace.si.edu/visit/
mall/
This museum showcases the history of
air and space exploration and

features the Apollo 11 Command
Module, the Albert Einstein
Planetarium, an observatory open to
the public, and much more.

WEB SITES

Due to the changing nature of Internet
links, Rosen Publishing has developed
an online list of Web sites related to the
subject of this book. This site is updated
regularly. Please use this link to access
the list:

http://www.rosenlinks.com/CORE/Magn

Abramson, Albert. *The History of Television, 1880 to 1941*. Jefferson, NC: McFarland Publishing, 2009.

Ascher, Kate. *The Heights: Anatomy of a Skyscraper*. New York: Penguin Books, 2014.

Bernanrd, Andreas. *Lifted: A Cultural History of the Elevator*. New York: NYU Press, 2014.

Blundell, Stephen. *Magnetism: A Very Short Introduction*. Oxford, UK: Oxford University Press, 2012.

Bodanis, David. *Electric Universe: How Electricity Switched on the Modern World*. New York: Broadway Books, 2006.

Bortolotti, Dan. *Auroras: Fire in the Sky*. Richmond Hill, Ontario, Canada: Firefly Books, 2012.

Coey, J. M. D. *Magnetism and Magnetic Materials*. Cambridge, UK: Cambridge University Press, 2010.

Gray, Charlotte. *Reluctant Genius: Alexander Graham Bell and the Passion for Invention*. New York: Arcade Publishing, 2011.

Gray, Theodore. *The Elements: A Visual Exploration of Every Known Atom in the Universe*. New York: Black Dog and Leventhal Publishers, 2012.

Hartman, Eve, and Wendy Meshbesher. *Magnetism and Electromagnets*. Sci-Hi: Physical Science. Chicago: Raintree, 2009.

Hochfelder, David. *The Telegraph in America, 1832–1920*. Baltimore, MD: Johns Hopkins University Press, 2013.

Hughes, Austin, and Bill Drury. *Electric Motors and Drives: Fundamentals, Types and Applications*. Waltham, MA: Newnes, 2013.

Laramie, James, and John Lowry. *Electric Vehicles Technology Explained*. Hoboken, NJ: Wiley, 2013.

Lincoln, Don. *The Quantum Frontier: The Large Hadron Collider*. Baltimore, MD: Johns Hopkins University Press, 2009.

Livingston, James. *Rising Force: The Magic of Magnetic Levitation*. Cambridge, MA: Harvard University Press, 2011.

Pol, Andri. *Inside CERN: European Organization for Nuclear Research*. Zurich, Switzerland: Lars Müller Publishers, 2014.

Purcell, Edward M., and David J. Morin. *Electricity and Magnetism*. Cambridge, UK: Cambridge University Press, 2013.

Saunders, Craig. *What is the Theory of Plate Tectonics?*. New York: Crabtree Publishing, 2011.

PHOTO CREDITS